Cambridge Elements ≡

Elements in Child Development
edited by
Marc H. Bornstein
National Institute of Child Health and Human Development, Bethesda
Institute for Fiscal Studies, London
UNICEF, New York City

SOCIALIZING CHILDREN

Joan E. Grusec
University of Toronto
Maayan Davidov
The Hebrew University of Jerusalem

CAMBRIDGE
UNIVERSITY PRESS

CAMBRIDGE
UNIVERSITY PRESS

University Printing House, Cambridge CB2 8BS, United Kingdom

One Liberty Plaza, 20th Floor, New York, NY 10006, USA

477 Williamstown Road, Port Melbourne, VIC 3207, Australia

314–321, 3rd Floor, Plot 3, Splendor Forum, Jasola District Centre, New Delhi – 110025, India

79 Anson Road, #06–04/06, Singapore 079906

Cambridge University Press is part of the University of Cambridge.

It furthers the University's mission by disseminating knowledge in the pursuit of education, learning, and research at the highest international levels of excellence.

www.cambridge.org
Information on this title: www.cambridge.org/9781108827034
DOI: 10.1017/9781108920780

First published 2021

A catalogue record for this publication is available from the British Library.

ISBN 978-1-108-82703-4 Paperback
ISSN 2632-9948 (online)
ISSN 2632-993X (print)

Socializing Children

Elements in Child Development

DOI: 10.1017/9781108920780
First published online: April 2021

Joan E. Grusec
University of Toronto

Maayan Davidov
The Hebrew University of Jerusalem

Author for correspondence: Joan E. Grusec, jgrusec@gmail.com

Abstract: Complaints are often made that recommendations about how to rear children are contradictory and, therefore, not helpful. In this Element we survey the history of theory and research relevant to childrearing in an attempt to show how apparent differences can be resolved. We suggest that socialization occurs in different domains, with each domain fostering socialization in a different way. Thus, there is no all-purpose principle or mechanism of socialization but, rather, different forms of relationship between child and agent that serve a different function, involve different rules for effecting behavior change, and facilitate different outcomes. Using this framework, we survey research relevant to different domains, including the roles played by parents, siblings, and peers in the socialization process. We follow this with a discussion of how culture and biology make their contribution to an understanding of domains of socialization.

Keywords: socialization, parenting, internalization, peer and sibling influence, biological factors

ISBNs: 9781108827034 (PB), 9781108920780 (OC)
ISSNs: 2632-9948 (online), 2632-993X (print)

Contents

1 Introduction

This Element surveys knowledge about the socialization process – that is, the ways in which individuals come to behave in accord with the standards, beliefs, values, and actions of their social group. Socialization happens whenever individuals enter a new social group – when, for example, they start a new job, become a parent, emigrate to a new country, or move into late adulthood. In this Element we focus, however, on the most important and most studied example of socialization – the preparation of children to successfully enter a world beyond the family. Noteworthy is the fact that socialization in all contexts is not a one-way street involving the straightforward transmission of standards and values from those who are more experienced to those who are less experienced (Kuczynski & Mol, 2015). Rather, new group members construct values from their socialization experiences. Additionally, new group members may alter the attitudes and behavior of older members of the group. In the case of the family, for example, children may urge their parents to stop using their cell phones while driving or to stop smoking or engaging in other unhealthy behaviors, or to change rules and requirements to something the children find more reasonable. It should be noted as well that where more than one socialization agent is involved, discrepant information about appropriate behavior may occur, requiring children to resolve the discrepancy.

In addition to the acquisition of standards of behavior, children need to learn how to control their emotions, including fear, anger, frustration, sadness, and excessive displays of pleasure. These emotions interfere with the display of socially appropriate actions and therefore must be managed. Also learned during the course of socialization are ways of resolving conflict, as well as attitudes toward relationships with others. Notably, socialization includes both the intentional efforts of socialization agents to guide children toward the acquisition of desired characteristics and behavior, as well as the influence that socialization agents unconsciously exert on children's development through the conditions they unwittingly create or the example they inadvertently provide. Moreover, socialization efforts and influences may be more or less effective in fostering children's positive development and adjustment (or, when very ineffective, children's maladjustment). A major goal for socialization theory and research has thus been to characterize how successful socialization of children occurs.

1.1 The Centrality of Parents

Several years ago, Harris (1995) created a stir among developmental scientists when she argued that groups external to the family had more influence on socialization of children than did parents. Scarr (1992), in a similar vein, had suggested that parental rearing had little impact on children's development unless it was extreme in its content. In fact, these were not totally novel ideas. Piaget (1932), for example, maintained that parents had a lesser role to play in moral development than did peers. This was because the authoritarian relationship children had with their parents meant that there was little opportunity for children to learn the importance of considering different points of view, an essential aspect of development.

The assertions of Harris and Scarr were important in reminding developmentalists about the wide range of influences on children's socialization. Indeed, parents are far from the only agents of socialization. Children themselves, of course, have an impact on their own socialization, not only because of their genetic predispositions but also because, as described earlier, they construct values and beliefs rather than simply taking over what they are being taught. Children are also exposed to siblings, grandparents, teachers, and peers from an early age, as well as to nonparental caregivers in the home. Finally, of course, and not insignificantly, television, social media, and video games can make significant contributions to the socialization process.

There are many good reasons, however, why parents are more important than any of these other socialization agents. First, parents are present in children's lives from the moment of birth (and even earlier), and thus relationships with parents are the earliest bonds that children form. Moreover, in most societies, responsibility for child care is formally assigned to parents or close relatives, often with legislated rights and responsibilities and with a reluctance on the part of the social group to intervene except in extreme cases of neglect or abuse. Moreover, whereas relationships with teachers and peers can be terminated, those with parents (usually) cannot. Another reason for parental prominence in childrearing is that parents have more opportunity to monitor their children on a continuing basis. Thus, they are in the best position to know what their children are doing and thinking and to react accordingly. Perhaps the most important reason for parents to have a leading position with respect to socialization is that they have to live with their children and interact with them on a continuing basis. Life is more pleasant when children are well behaved and cooperative, and so the motive to facilitate good behavior and cooperation is substantial.

1.1.1 Evolution of Parental Socialization

Evolutionary theory provides another way of understanding the primacy of parents and the family in the socialization process. Socialization, in the sense of an extended period of immaturity during which children receive intensive care and guidance in preparation for maturity, can be viewed as an evolutionary adaptation. Fossil evidence indicates that a substantial increase in brain size occurred during human evolution, with cranial capacity more than tripling in size. This dramatic increase in brain size is largely attributed to the growing social complexity of human society, which included competition and cooperation over resources and status, within and between social groups (Flinn, 2017; Flinn et al., 2005). Larger brains, with bigger cortexes, enabled more advanced cognitive abilities, particularly social cogitation and communication skills, which were vital for successfully coping with these social challenges. However, due to the limitations of the woman's birth canal size, expanded brain sizes meant more altricial infants – that is, infants physically immature and helpless at birth, with substantial brain growth and maturation occurring postnatally. Moreover, the social complexities of group living required the teaching and fostering of children's social competencies so that they could cope with the challenges they were likely to face later on. An extended period of socialization is therefore an evolutionary adaptation which enabled considerable brain development during childhood, the protection and nurturing of physically immature children, and the appropriate preparation of the young for the complexities of social life (Flinn, 2017; Flinn et al., 2005).

Dependent children require intensive caregiving over many years. In our evolutionary history, such caregiving of the young was primarily provided by the family which, in addition to mothers, included fathers as well as other relatives. Notably, whereas mothers have absolute certainty that their children are their biological offspring, fathers do not. Male–female pair bonding is therefore seen as an important evolutionary adaptation that increased fathers' certainty regarding their biological paternity, and which therefore facilitated paternal investment in caring for their young (Bugental et al., 2015; Flinn, 2017). Caring for and nurturing offspring is crucial for children's reproductive fitness, but can be demanding and taxing for caregivers. Humans (both females and males) have therefore evolved a strong motivation to care for children. This evolved tendency is rooted in human biology, including brain functioning and hormones (see Section 8 of this Element).

1.2 Internalization

Many socialization theorists see internalization of values and attitudes as the primary goal of childrearing. Children must comply with societal values and directives not because they fear punishment for unacceptable behavior or because they hope for reward in the case of acceptable behavior, but because they have come to see the inherent correctness of a particular point of view or requirement. Attribution theorists (Lepper, 1983), calling on the "minimal sufficiency principle," have argued that internalization is facilitated when socialization involves discipline that is just sufficient to produce positive social behavior –that is, uses the optimal amount of pressure: not too little (as no change in behavior will occur), yet not too much (as no internalization will occur). When the pressure to conform is no more than necessary to obtain compliance, then the resulting positive behavior will less likely be attributed to external pressures. Instead, it would more likely be attributed to a belief in the intrinsic correctness of the behavior. As a result, even in the absence of surveillance, the behavior will endure.

Social Determination Theory (SDT) has much to say about internalization (Ryan & Deci, 2017). The proposal here is that, rather than being merely absent or present, there is a continuum of internalization. This continuum begins with external reasons or motivations for behavior – fear of punishment or hope of reward. Next is introjected – the achievement of self-approval by pleasing others or avoiding shame or guilt. Finally are identified – action taken in accord with personally important and valued goals, and integrated – adoption of a behavior that is in accord with a broader belief system about the self and that thus contributes to a coherent and cohesive system of values. One important feature of socialization that is central to internalization according to SDT is autonomy support. Thus, children are more likely to move closer to the integrated end of the internalization continuum when their need for autonomy is being supported. Autonomy-supportive agents provide meaningful rationales for limits and demands, give choice and opportunities for initiative-taking within these limits, and acknowledge children's feelings (Grolnick & Pomerantz, 2009; Grolnick & Ryan, 1989). More generally, autonomy-supportive agents are empathic, descriptive (i.e., informational instead of evaluative), and take the perspective of the child. They also provide opportunities for the child to actively participate in decision-making or problem-solving, instead of being intrusive, dominating, and pressuring.

Another conceptualization of internalization comes from social cognitive approaches to development and, in particular, from the work of Vygotsky (1978). Vygotsky argued that higher skills, both cognitive and social, are acquired in interactions with more knowledgeable others. The adult (or more knowledgeable person), working within the child's current level of understanding or "zone of proximal development," gradually guides that child to adopt more advanced ways of thinking. This occurs by creating shared understanding (intersubjectivity) regarding the matter at hand (task, topic, etc.), enabling the child to adopt and internalize the adult's more complex way of thinking and reasoning.

2 Overview

This Element begins with a detailed description of how theories of socialization have developed over many years to yield current ways of viewing the socialization process – ways that often lead to contradictory recommendations with respect to effective parenting. We suggest that these contradictions can be resolved by positing that socialization happens in many different contexts or domains that require different forms of intervention. We next move to a discussion of how parents' beliefs about themselves and their children influence their socialization practices, and provide a brief survey of the important role played by siblings and peers in the socialization process. This is followed by a discussion of how culture and biology facilitate further understanding of socialization. Last, we offer some final observations about the socialization process.

3 Approaches to Understanding Socialization: How Did We Get from Freud to Present-Day Formulations?

Studies of socialization have been guided by many different theoretical formulations, not all of which appear to be compatible. In this section we first describe the major theoretical approaches to socialization. In Section 4 we attempt to bring together research findings they have generated in an organized manner, which can help resolve some of the contradictions they appear to pose.

3.1 Psychoanalytic Theory

Modern views of childrearing can largely be traced back to Freud. In *Civilization and its discontents* (S. Freud, 1930), Freud argued that children experience anger and resentment in the course of being taught acceptable behavior if strict demands are placed on them. Fear of abandonment or, at least, loss of love, however, keeps them from expressing their hostility. Instead, they repress the hostility and adopt parental rules as their own – that is, they internalize the rules. This internalization includes self-punishment or guilt, which motivates adoption of parental standards and promotes acceptable behavior even when sources of external disapproval and punishment are no longer present. An important feature of Freud's thinking was the emphasis on fear of loss of love as a primary motivator for adopting parental directives. Another important feature was that these directives were adopted without change: values and attitudes were seen to be transmitted to, rather than constructed by, the child.

Freud's thinking became particularly influential in North America after he accepted an invitation to lecture at Clark University in 1909. The ideas he presented had considerable appeal because of their richness and complexity, although the reception among practitioners was more positive than that among academics (Sears, 1975). In the 1930s, psychoanalysis became a North American specialty when many analysts were forced to flee from Germany.

3.2 Behaviorism

In academic circles, ideas relevant to children's social development were more likely to involve classical conditioning, with an emphasis on behavior. Thus, the works of Pavlov and Watson composed the dominant approach. Watson (1925) maintained that the ability to modify behavior through environmental manipulation and, in particular, through the process of classical conditioning, was virtually boundless. He wrote:

> Give me a dozen healthy infants, well-formed and my own world to bring them up in and I'll guarantee to bring any one at random and train him to become any type of specialist I might select – doctor, lawyer, artist, merchant-chief and, yes, even beggar-man and thief – regardless of his talents, penchants, tendencies, abilities, vocation, and race of his ancestors. (1925, p. 104)

The behaviorist approach was welcomed in the North American context given that North America, and the United States in particular, was a society founded on rugged individualism and focused on action as opposed to thinking and reflection (Buss, 1975). Behaviorism also appealed to academic psychologists because it was based on carefully conducted research. Behaviorism flourished with the work of Skinner, who focused on instrumental or operant conditioning and the role of reinforcement in this learning. Skinner also continued with the strong emphasis in North American psychology on the importance of studying behavior rather than the mind.

3.3 Social Learning Theory

Hullian learning theory provided a further guide for the role of conditioning principles in development. Hull's approach centered on the learning of associations between unconditioned and conditioned stimuli, and on drive reduction as the primary reinforcement for behavior. It was this approach that provided the framework for social learning theory.

Psychoanalytic practitioners argued that the principles of Freudian theory were not amenable to scientific testing and had to be assessed through the free association of patients undergoing psychoanalysis or through the observation of children during structured play sessions. However, a group of influential researchers located at the Yale Institute of Human Development tried to test psychoanalytic hypotheses by translating them into the concepts of conditioning and drive reduction (e.g., Dollard et al., 1939). A number of corresponding features of the two approaches made this possible. Thus, drive reduction was important for both theories. Freud's pleasure principle and reinforcement were similar. So too were the concepts of displacement (focusing on a new but similar object or goal because the original is too anxiety-provoking) and generalization (responding in the same way to similar stimuli). Additionally, but not surprisingly, similar behavioral outcomes were the object of their interest, viz., dependency, aggression, and identification or incorporation of parental standards (Grusec, 1992).

Sears (e.g., 1963) argued that mothers become secondarily reinforcing because of their association with primary drive reduction in the form of feeding and provision of physical comfort. In this way a dependency motive develops. Sears went further, suggesting that because young children are not able to discriminate between themselves and their mothers, they reproduce or imitate her behavior to satisfy their dependency needs. Unclear, however, was why mothers should be imitated when dependency needs were not activated, and so this particular set of hypotheses was abandoned (Grusec, 1992). Nevertheless, the research undertaken by Sears and his colleagues provided the base for future investigations of childrearing. Sears et al. (1957), for example, interviewed 379 mothers about their childrearing practices and the effects of these practices. They focused on discipline, which included punishment, withdrawal of love, and reasoning, and found that children's conscience or internalization of parental standards of conduct was higher in those whose mothers used withdrawal of love and who were warm – that is, had love they could withdraw. Sears et al. suggested that withdrawal of love required the child to imitate maternal behavior to compensate for its loss. The topics Sears et al. studied – dependency, aggression, conscience development, and sex-role behaviors – remain topics of interest to this day.

3.3.1 Bidirectionality

Another contribution made by Sears was to point out that the relationship between mother and child is bidirectional (Sears, 1951). Not only do parents have an effect on their children's development, children's behavior also has an impact on what their parents do: both parents and children are subject to the laws of learning. This idea was emphasized again in Bell's (1968) classic paper, which illustrated how links between parenting and child outcomes typically interpreted as parental effects could just as easily be viewed as stemming from child effects. Nevertheless, this is a feature of socialization about which researchers still need to be reminded (Kuczynski & Mol, 2015), no doubt because they are more interested in giving advice to parents about how to affect the behavior of children than they are in giving advice to children about how to affect the behavior of their parents (Davidov et al., 2015). Parents do a much better job, however, when they understand how they themselves are affected by the actions of their children.

3.3.2 Other-oriented Induction

Further elaboration of Sears' categories of discipline was provided by Hoffman (1970). He distinguished power assertion, love withdrawal, and induction as features of discipline, with induction being the provision of explanation and appeals to the child's pride and desire to be mature. A particularly important aspect of discipline was "other-oriented" induction or pointing out the negative impact of the child's behavior on another person. In a review of existing studies, Hoffman found that, on average, power assertion in the form of physical punishment, deprivation of privileges, and application of force or threats of those reactions was negatively related to the development of conscience or internalization, whereas withdrawal of love was unrelated. Induction, particularly other-oriented induction, was positively related to conscience development. Warmth was also a predictor of positive outcomes. These relations held for mothers but not for fathers, at least in the few studies that were then available.

Hoffman proposed that power-assertive discipline techniques make the child angry because they challenge the child's autonomy, as well as provide a model of antisocial behavior. A power-assertive approach to discipline also focuses the child's attention on the self rather than the individual being harmed, thereby failing to make use of the child's empathic ability. Love withdrawal can be more effective, but generates anxiety that can detract from the child's ability to internalize the message. Other-oriented induction, in contrast, utilizes the child's empathic ability by maintaining focus on the other, is potentially less anxiety-provoking, and provides information about how one should behave and why. Hoffman (1982) noted, however, that a moderate level of power assertion or disapproval is required to gain the child's attention and ensure the message contained in induction is heard.

3.4 Social Cognitive Theory

Sears had great difficulty explaining how children learn new responses by imitating their mothers. Skinner (1953) had similar problems with imitation and had resorted to suggesting that children learn novel responses by successive approximation, a process requiring that elements of a new response be reinforced as they grew closer and closer in form to the desired outcome. Bandura and Walters (1963) noted, however, that this was an unnecessarily cumbersome approach to learning: no one would teach an adolescent to drive a car by means of trial-and-error procedures, nor would one entrust a firearm to an armed services recruit without a demonstration of how it should be handled. Noting that the learning of new responses could be achieved simply through observing the behavior of others, even if observed actions were not enacted, they maintained that observational learning was a form of learning that did not need to rely on other principles of learning. Indeed, they suggested that observational learning had a primary position among mechanisms of learning, given its efficiency as a way of teaching new behaviors.

Bandura and Walters referred to the centrality of observational learning as reflecting a "sociobehavioristic" approach, thereby emphasizing the fact that this form of learning was a social process. The label was modified again as Bandura (Bandura, 1986) began to refer to the approach as a social cognitive one. This change in labeling was appropriate, given that events required for successful learning through observation went beyond behavior, including attention to a model's actions, retention of viewed material in memory in either an imaginal or verbal form, conversion of these representations into actions similar to those originally modeled, and, finally, an incentive to motivate the matching of behavior. The emphasis on cognition can also be seen in Bandura's explanation for internalization or the shifting of control over behavior from external agents to the self. He argued that by observing models, being taught directly, and experiencing reactions of others to their behavior, children learn to self-regulate or set standards for their own behavior. They do not passively take over the model's standards but, instead, make choices. Thus, value systems are constructed, not transmitted as Freud and Sears had maintained. Variables affecting children's choice of what to model include how similar they see themselves to the model, the extent to which they see behavior as a function of their own efforts and abilities, and their perceived competence to reproduce the model's behavior.

3.5 Applied Behavior Analysis and Coercion Theory

Bandura remains a prominent figure in psychology. Additionally, however, researchers and practitioners continued to apply straightforward reinforcement principles to a wide variety of learning situations, including the modification of psychotic behavior (Ayllon & Michael, 1959), the use of tokens to reward classroom learning (Bijou & Baer, 1961), and treatment of autistic children (Lovaas et al., 1973).

Patterson and his colleagues produced impressive results in their interventions directed at antisocial and delinquent behavior. In what they label "coercion theory," they describe the bidirectional nature of troubled mother–child interactions, with challenged mothers unintentionally reinforcing children's negative or difficult behaviors by giving in when those negative behaviors reach an intolerable level. Children escalate behavior to maximum intensity early in the exchange, whereas mothers escalate their behavior more slowly and then withdraw as early as possible. In this way mothers negatively reinforce their children's antisocial behavior by ceasing their own, and so they inadvertently train their children to be more aversive by ceasing their own aversive behavior (Patterson, 1982). In this analysis children are clearly active seekers and selectors of caregiver interventions, as opposed to passive recipients of interventions. Another feature of Patterson's approach was his dismissal of the need for a concept of internalization. Patterson (1997), for example, suggested that the complexity of moment-to-moment experience makes it unlikely that the experience can be mentally processed and, therefore, internalized.

Interventions based on principles of behavior analysis continue to be successful in the treatment of antisocial and delinquent behavior (Forgatch & Gewirtz, 2017), with an emphasis on positive and negative reinforcement, limit setting or discipline, monitoring, family problem-solving, and positive involvement with the child. The use of these techniques avoids coercive interactions and negative reinforcement, which are features of many troubled families.

3.6 Attachment Theory

Object relations theory (Klein, 1952), an offshoot of psychoanalytic thinking, provided the base for attachment theory. According to Klein, early family experiences shape social development, but such shaping is motivated by the need for contact and formation of relationships with others, rather than sex, aggression, or secondary drives (as would be suggested by psychoanalytic or social learning theories). Theorizing about this basic need to form relationships accorded with the work of Lorenz (1970) on imprinting, which showed that many bird species instinctively bond with the first moving object that they see. Added to this was the research of Harlow (1958), demonstrating that rhesus monkeys preferred to cling to cloth-covered surrogate mothers over wire-covered ones, even when the latter were a source of food and should, according to a social learning analysis, have been more attractive.

The idea that positive relationships were a basic need, rather than a result of learning, was transformed by Bowlby (1958) into a theory about childhood security. According to attachment theory, humans have evolved to favor maintenance of a close physical relationship between mother and child. Their exploration of the world is facilitated if they have a secure base to which they know they can return if they feel anxious. When children experience a dangerous situation or feel unsafe, the attachment system is aroused and they move back to the attachment figure. When the caregiver acknowledges the child's needs for comfort and protection, as well as the need for independent exploration of the environment, the child develops an internal working model of the self as valued and competent (Bowlby, 1973). Bowlby's emphasis on children's actual experiences with caregivers, as opposed to children's fantasy life, led to a clash with the psychoanalytic establishment of the time (e.g., A. Freud, 1960).

Bowlby's research was conducted at the Tavistock Clinic in London. There he studied the effects on children of being separated from their mothers, producing, with Robertson, a series of films that made it very clear how distressing such separation is, even for children who have a positive relationship with their parent. In 1950, Bowlby was joined at the Tavistock by Ainsworth who, several years later, conducted one of the most influential studies in developmental science (the "Baltimore study"; Ainsworth et al., 1978). In that study, her hypothesis that caregivers who responded immediately to their babies' crying during the first year of life would have babies who cried less when they were a year old was supported; the outcome, of course, was the opposite of what would have been predicted by a reinforcement theorist. Ainsworth (Ainsworth & Bell, 1970) also devised the Strange Situation, which measures how the 12- to 18-month child's attachment system is organized vis-à-vis a particular caregiver. Three groups of children were identified on the basis of their behavior on being reunited with their mother after separation. Secure babies were pleased and relieved to reunite with the caregiver, whereas insecure babies appeared either to be uncaring (actively avoiding the mother) or to be upset and not able to be consoled. Ainsworth also expanded on Bowlby's basic notion of responsiveness to crying or distress as necessary for the development of secure attachment: she found that secure attachment was related to maternal sensitive responding, which included maternal acceptance, responsiveness to signals, nonintrusiveness, and accessibility.

Attachment theory continues to be a significant force in developmental science. Thompson (2016) noted that there have been three stages of research guided by the theory. First was the demonstration that early attachment relationships are stable over time and predict later psychosocial functioning, such as positive peer social relationships and cooperativeness. Next came many studies exploring aspects of later behavior associated with early attachment security. These ranged from social skills, social cognition, behavior problems, language development, and achievement to political ideology and IQ – outcomes far from what Bowlby had originally envisioned. This stage of research often had no underlying theory and failed to consider mediating variables that might account for linkages. In a third stage, attachment researchers are now addressing plausible mediating variables to understand the multiple connections that exist between security status and child outcomes. In his review of attachment theory, Thompson noted how attachment theory has been substantially altered in light of increased understanding of children's cognitive and behavioral sophistication, as well as advances in genetics, evolutionary biology, and developmental neuroscience. Because of this, he argued that attachment theory should be seen as a foundation for new thinking about early parent–child relationships.

3.7 Reciprocity

Parent–child reciprocity occurs when caregivers go along with reasonable requests from their children and children, in turn, go along with reasonable requests from their parents. Thus Maccoby and Martin (1983) proposed that children's willingness to engage in this sort of exchange was a mediator between a parent's requests for compliance and children's willingness to take a receptive and cooperative stance toward those requests. In contrast to the negative emotions associated with discipline and attachment – guilt and distress, respectively – reciprocity is based on more positive emotions, such as pleasure. It differs from discipline and conflict because there is no disagreement between the child and the socializing agent, and it differs from secure attachment because there is no anxiety or distress on the part of the child.

In support of their proposal, Parpal and Maccoby (1985) found that mothers trained to follow their child's lead during play by complying with their child's suggestions and directives, as well as refraining from commands and criticism, were better able to get their child to comply with subsequent requests than were mothers who were simply instructed to play with their child as they usually did. Further, Lay et al. (1989) demonstrated that children whose mothers had been compliant were more likely to be in a happy mood that presumably made them more receptive to requests from their mother. Maccoby (1983), in underlining the positive aspects of reciprocity, suggested that a caregiver who had been responsive to their child had "put assets into the socialization bank – assets that can be drawn upon when the child has developed to the point when socialization pressures are necessary" (p. 363).

3.8 Cognitive Approaches: Social Construction

By the early 1970s, behaviorism was no longer a dominant force in most areas of developmental science. Instead, interest focused on the mental underpinnings of behavior. The Russian psychologist Vygotsky (1978), for example, argued that cognitive growth occurs in a social context which affects the form that knowledge takes: higher cognitive skills emerge from social interactions with those who are more competent, such as parents, teachers, and older siblings. Vygotsky also emphasized the cultural aspect of this process. Thus, in each social context, children will learn and internalize different ways of thinking and acting, depending on the practices, beliefs, and values characteristic of their social group. Acquisition of knowledge comes from collaborative dialogues with individuals in the child's environment who have greater knowledge. Vygotsky used the term "zone of proximal development" to describe the context in which learning occurs. This zone is the area between what children are capable of doing on their own and what they can do with guidance from or collaboration with others who have greater ability. The zone shifts continuously as new levels of sophistication are reached. The eventual goal is internalization, wherein child and teacher have reached a shared understanding: the child has taken on the teacher's view as their own (Puntambekar & Hübscher, 2005).

The notion of "scaffolding" supplements that of zones of proximal development (Wood et al., 1976). Teachers support or scaffold the learning of their students. However, as those students become more proficient this support can be gradually reduced. As scaffolding is lessened, students are then able to complete a task on their own. As with scaffolding that supports the construction of a building, so too is scaffolding of learning lessened as work is completed and help from others is no longer needed. When learning is going well teachers become less specific in their help, and, when learning is going less well, their assistance becomes more frequent and specific.

3.9 Social Psychology

What is likely the most significant view of socialization has come not from developmental science, but from social psychology. At the beginning of World War II, Lewin, a German psychologist, studied reactions to autocratic direction (Lewin et al., 1939). Boys participated in recreational and craft groups that were run either by authoritarian leaders who were aloof and dictatorial, democratic leaders who encouraged group decision-making and were rational and dispassionate, or laissez-faire leaders who were friendly but nondirective. Most successful at working well in the absence of the leader was the democratic group. Baldwin (1955) applied these findings to an analysis of parenting styles, expanding the democratic style to include warmth. Baumrind (1971, 2012) elaborated further in an analysis that continues to be influential to the present day. She distinguished authoritative parenting, which included imposition of high standards, reasoning, negotiation, responsiveness, and encouragement of autonomy; authoritarian parenting, characterized by high demands, strictness, and low responsiveness to the child's situation; and permissive parenting, which was overly responsive to the child's demands and inconsistent in rule enforcement. These various styles reflected attitudes toward the child that created an emotional climate in which learning occurred, with the authoritative style most conducive to social responsibility, peer competence, cooperation with adults, social dominance, nonconformity, and purposiveness (Maccoby, 2015), particularly in Western cultural contexts (Chao, 2001).

4 Putting it All Together: A Domains Approach to Socialization

The various approaches to socialization we have just described are not always consistent in the recommendations they make about what is effective socialization. Should crying children be comforted, or should their crying be ignored? Should parents gain compliance by responding to their children's requests, or should they use power assertion and reasoning in response to their children's noncompliance? Do rewards and punishments promote good behavior, or do they challenge the child's autonomy? Should a parent talk to a child about the importance of behaving well, or is it better to wait and respond to the child's bad behavior? Different approaches provide different answers. One way of making sense of these different answers is to adopt a domains of socialization approach (see, for example, Grusec & Davidov, 2010, 2015, 2019).

Following a lead provided by Bugental (2000) and colleagues (Bugental & Goodnow, 1998; Bugental & Grusec, 2006), Grusec and Davidov argued that different caregiver–child interactions constitute different socialization contexts, or domains, as they provide children with different learning experiences involved in acquiring a variety of important abilities, knowledge, values, and skills. In the course of everyday interactions, specific domains are activated as a function of the demands of the situation and the needs and motives of the interaction partners, with effective parenting taking different forms in each domain. Thus, each domain differs in its evolutionary and biological underpinnings, developmental course, rules of interaction, and the nature of the socialization tasks involved. Because parent–child interactions are modular, different domains foster socialization in a different way. Accordingly, there is no all-purpose mechanism involved in socialization. Rather, what is appropriate depends on the domain in which parent and child currently find themselves.

Grusec and Davidov identified five domains, reflecting the mechanisms identified by various socialization researchers as reviewed earlier. These were: protection – comfort and support for a distressed child and equipping that child to self-soothe; reciprocity – development of a cooperative and mutually compliant relationship; control – discipline when a child has misbehaved or positive reward for desired behavior; guided learning – acquiring knowledge through scaffolded teaching; and group participation – learning by observing other group members perform valued activities and actively participating in customs and activities important for the group. The roles played by caregiver and child also differ as a function of domain: these are, in turn, distressed child and responsive caregiver in the protection domain, equal status partners in the reciprocity domain, hierarchical relationship in the control domain, teacher–student in the guided learning domain, and members of the same social group in the group participation domain. Each of these domains, of course, emerges from each of the various approaches described in Section 3 of this Element. Protection links to attachment theory, reciprocity to work on parent–child exchange of favors, guided learning to social construction, and group participation to Bandura's social cognitive approach. Control has been by far the most studied feature of socialization and includes social learning theory, applied behavior analysis and other related approaches, as well as Baumrind's identification of parenting styles.

The first two domains – protection and reciprocity – address the nature of the relationship between parent and child, and the next three domains concern different ways in which attitudes, values, and social behaviors are acquired. Protection and reciprocity therefore provide the relational foundation upon which control, guided learning, and group participation interactions further build. Effective parenting does not involve doing the same thing at all times but, rather, adjusting interventions to the particular domain in which the child is currently operating. Attachment theory, social learning theory, social cognitive theory, social construction theory, and parenting styles each become a guide for action depending on the state of the child. A domains of socialization approach, then, is defined by features of the parent–child interaction and not by the outcome.

4.1 Foundations of Socialization Effectiveness: Protection and Reciprocity

4.1.1 Protection

Bowlby argued that children have evolved to seek their caregivers for protection when they are in some form of danger involving fear, anxiety, a threat to life, or distress. Similarly, caregivers have evolved to respond to the child's distress. In this way the survival and reproductive success of both members of the dyad is promoted. The protection domain, then, comes into play whenever children feel insecure: hurt, frightened, ill, in danger, or distressed. In this domain parents or others serve as secure bases from which their children can explore the world. Although Thompson (2016) as noted earlier (Section 3.6) argued that attachment theory should be seen as a foundation for new thinking about early parent–child relationships, it can also be argued that the uniqueness of attachment theory is found in Bowlby's original thesis that protection and security are the foundation of personality development (Bowlby,1958,1982). When children are young, trust in a caregiver to keep them from harm facilitates their exploration of the world, secure in the knowledge that they can retreat to a safe place if they need to. Caregivers who are successful in making children feel secure are reasonably comforting but not overly solicitous. As well, they are not dismissive or punitive when children display distress. They also take into account individual differences in children's fearfulness. Thus, temperamentally fearful children do better when their parents are more challenging in reaction to that timidity (Degnan et al., 2008; Hastings et al., 2014). This tailoring of responses to children's distress reflects the position that mothers should be "good enough" in their socialization practices by gradually withdrawing support and forcing the child to compensate for the parent's apparent failure (Winnicott, 1953). It also highlights the notion of "goodness of fit" – the idea that effective parenting must take into account children's temperamental characteristics, current needs, and capabilities.

Caregivers who respond effectively to their children's distress and anxiety and help them deal with these emotions also facilitate the development of their children's empathy. When caregivers comfort appropriately, children learn to cope not only with their own negative affect but that of others as well. Feeling the same negative emotion as another or, in a later manifestation, having a sympathetic reaction to that distress, motivates behavior that is designed to alleviate another individual's suffering (Eisenberg et al., 2015). Additionally, understanding how others are feeling is an important mechanism underlying conscience development because it leads to better understanding of the emotional impact of one's harmful behaviors on others (see Hoffman, 1970).

Although empathy and sympathy are motivators of prosocial behavior, levels of these emotions that are too high can lead to personal distress and an urge to escape from an unpleasant situation. Eisenberg et al. (2019), for example, reported that mothers who distracted their children from feelings of distress or discussed ways of dealing with distress had toddlers who showed greater comforting or helping attempts toward an adult in apparent distress. Mothers who were less supportive had children who were more likely to display personal distress by going to their mothers for comfort, thereby ignoring the individual who was in need of help.

Responsiveness to Distress and Warmth. Responsiveness to distress should be distinguished from warmth. They are separate entities, comprising different and distinct features of the parent–child relationship. Responsiveness to distress involves reactions to children's negative emotions, whereas warmth is generally considered to be the expression of positive affect, affection, and pleasure in interactions with children. These two components of socialization are different in their features and outcomes (Goldberg et al., 1999). Responsiveness to distress, for example, is found in all cultures, whereas parental warmth is not (MacDonald, 1992). Fox and Davidson (1987) found that separation protest was associated with right frontal brain activation, whereas the pleasure elicited by a mother's approach and reaching for her infant was associated with left frontal brain activation. In a study that included both mothers and fathers, Davidov and Grusec (2006) noted that responsiveness to distress, but not warmth, predicted children's competent regulation of negative affect (e.g., ability to recover quickly from upset or distress). For mothers, warmth, but not responsiveness to distress, was a predictor of children's ability to regulate positive affect and, for boys, peer acceptance. In a sample of German children, responsiveness to distress was positively related to children's internalization of rules of conduct, whereas maternal warmth was positively related to children's level of effortful control (von Suchodoletz et al., 2011). In a longitudinal study, Wright et al. (2018) found that both maternal sensitivity to distress and positive regard made independent contributions to children's callous-unemotional traits and that they also interacted, so that the risk for high callous-unemotional traits arose from a combination of low sensitivity to distress and low positive regard. In another investigation of children's callous-unemotional traits, Humphreys et al. (2015) reported that observed sensitivity to distress at 30 and 42 months of age, but not warmth, was a negative predictor of callous-unemotional traits in early adolescence.

4.1.2 Reciprocity

From an evolutionary perspective, the strong tendency to assist others and receive favors in return is important for survival and reproductive success

(Hamilton, 1964). Even if the other is not biologically related, this assistance promotes survival. If favors are not reciprocated, then assistance stops. Whereas in protection situations the parent functions as a stronger and wiser provider of support, in reciprocity situations parent and child interact temporarily as equal status partners complying with each other's reasonable requests. These experiences of equality within the caregiver–child relationship increase the likelihood that children will continue to go along with the guidance and wishes of a socializing agent. Children's compliance in this situation is "receptive" as opposed to "situational," with compliance willingly given rather than coerced. As a result, a more generally compliant relationship is encouraged, where children see the needs and desires of agents of socialization as legitimate. The impact of reciprocity on compliance is demonstrated in a study by Kochanska et al. (2013) who, following Parpal and Maccoby (1985), trained mothers over the course of ten weeks to follow their toddler's lead and to be positive and rewarding. These toddlers, as well as those in a control group in which mothers had been instructed to play in their normal fashion, showed greater compliance with maternal requests compared to their baseline levels. Improvement continued at a 6-month follow-up, however, only for those in the training group.

Several researchers have expanded on Maccoby's original conception of reciprocity. Kochanska (1997) wrote about a mutually responsive orientation between parent and child, and Aksan et al. (2006) pointed out the importance of shared routines and understanding, harmonious communication, and expressions of affection and pleasure in the parent–child interaction. Synchrony is a term that has also been used to describe positive social interactions between parent and child (Feldman, 2012; Lindsey et al., 2009). These interactions include sharing the same focus of attention and mirroring each other's emotional state; sharing emotions, including smiles, laughter, sadness, and anger; mutual initiation of interactions; and mutual compliance. Positive outcomes of mutuality/synchrony include better self-regulation (Lindsey et al., 2009), prosocial behavior (Lindsey et al., 2010), reduction of behavior problems (Criss et al., 2003; Gardner et al., 2003), and conscience development (Kochanska et al., 2008). Importantly, effects in this domain are often specific. For example, mothers' responsiveness to their children's vocalizations is a predictor of language development but not quality of play, whereas responsiveness to play predicts quality of play but not language development (Bornstein & Tamis-Lemonda, 1997).

Following the Child's Lead vs. Mutuality.   Is there a difference in outcomes associated with mothers' allowing their children to take the lead in interactions and those associated with mutual, synchronous play or interaction? Are these the same events? In a study of early elementary school children, Davidov et al. (in press) compared mothers who co-led the play interaction with their child in a balanced, synchronous way with mothers who followed their child's lead. The two forms of reciprocity were associated with greater cooperation for different children. Following the child's lead was linked to greater cooperation for children viewed by mothers as difficult to manage, but made no difference for easy-to-manage children; the opposite pattern was found for sharing the lead, which was linked to greater cooperation only for easy-to-manage children. Differences also emerged when teachers were asked to rate the same children on their following of rules and their cooperation in the classroom: here these behaviors were associated with mothers' following the lead but not with mothers' sharing the lead. It would seem, then, that reciprocity takes on different meanings depending on how it is manifested.

Reciprocity and Responsiveness to Distress. Just as responsiveness to distress and warmth are distinct, so too are responsiveness to distress and reciprocity. Thus, maternal responsiveness to distress at 6 months predicted attachment security at 15 months, but responsiveness to nondistressing events such as social gestures did not (McElwain & Booth-Laforce, 2006). Leerkes et al. (2012) noted that the two forms of responsiveness serve different socialization goals. Sensitivity to distress centers around comfort and protection, whereas sensitivity to nondistress centers around reciprocity and learning. The two forms of responsiveness are modestly positively correlated, but they have different antecedents, with parental age, level of education, marital situation, and involvement of a father predictive of nondistress responsiveness but not of distress responsiveness (Leerkes et al., 2012). There are other indicants of the importance of distinguishing between responsiveness to distressing and to nondistressing events. For example, mothers who know what their children find comforting when they are distressed do not necessarily know what their children's interests and activities are (Vinik et al., 2011). There are also hormonal differences that are relevant to the distinction. Cortisol, for example, is related to stress or anxiety activated by early conditions of social deprivation (Fries et al., 2008). In contrast, oxytocin is associated with synchronous parent–child interaction (Priel et al., 2019; see also Section 7.3 of this Element).

4.2 Acquiring Values, Attitudes, and Socially Acceptable Behavior

Protection and reciprocity provide the base for socialization. The ability to act in accord with societal demands is further learned in the next three domains: control, which includes both discipline for antisocial behavior and reward for positive behavior; group participation; and guided learning.

4.2.1 Control

It is important for social groups to have rules of conduct that are obeyed in order that harmony can be achieved and harmful conflict avoided (Boehm, 2000). This acceptance of rules is accomplished in the control domain, where there is a vertical relationship between those with greater control over resources who can therefore ensure conformity on the part of those with lesser control. Parental control includes discipline in the form of power assertion and withdrawal of love, along with reasoning when rules are violated. It also includes reward for good behavior. We begin with a discussion of discipline in its various forms, and then move to consider reward for good behavior.

Discipline. Although other theoretical approaches have largely replaced that of social learning theory, Sears' emphasis on types of discipline has remained. Thus, research has been directed toward further elaboration of relations between forms of discipline and socialization outcomes. Grusec and Goodnow (1994), for example, noted a large number of studies showing the differential impact of discipline as a function of children's age, sex, and temperament; nature of the misdeed under consideration; cultural context; and whether the agent of socialization was male or female. They argued for the importance of distinguishing among different forms of power assertion (physical punishment, social isolation, withdrawal of privileges, shame), which had different effects, as well as different forms of reasoning (other-oriented, statements of norms, explanations that the child does not understand or does not accept), which also had different effects. Their conclusion was that the impact of any form of discipline or control was determined both by a child's accurate perception of the socializing agent's message and by the child's willingness to accept that message. Without both of these, successful socialization would not occur: a message might be heard correctly but not accepted, or a message might be heard incorrectly and this incorrect information accepted. Accurate perception requires that an agent of socialization delivers a message in a way that is appropriate for the child's age, that it is clear and consistent, and that the child's attention is captured by – for example, moderate levels of power assertion. Acceptance of the message is facilitated by the existence of a positive relationship with the agent of socialization, as well as by the extent to which the message is seen as reasonable and as self-generated. A number of studies have pointed to the usefulness of this analysis (e.g., Barni et al., 2011; Knafo & Schwartz, 2003; Padilla-Walker, 2007).

Grusec and Goodnow (1994) also pointed out that effective mothers do not use a single style of discipline when dealing with their child's misbehavior. Rather, they vary their discipline intervention according to the nature of the social standard their child has violated (Grusec & Kuczynski, 1980; Trickett &

Kuczynski, 1986). Thus, they respond differently to misdeeds such as lying and stealing, failure to show concern for others, lapses in impulse control, and violation of social conventions.

Power Assertion. Power assertion comes in many forms, not all of which are equivalent in their effects. The form most frequently discussed is physical punishment, with strong opinions expressed about its usefulness or its harmfulness (Baumrind & Thompson, 2002; Straus, 1996). The research evidence against the use of physical punishment is fairly persuasive, however. It is true that adverse effects of physical punishment are more frequent in European American children than in African American children (Lansford et al., 2004), with externalizing problems lesser in the latter group. The explanation offered is that physical punishment is more normative and acceptable in African American families and it is therefore interpreted by children as fair and appropriate rather than as a loss of self-control by a parent. Similarly, in countries with low use of physical punishment, the association between parental use of physical punishment and children's behavior problems is greater than in countries where physical punishment is more prevalent and seen as acceptable (see also the discussion of cultural influences on socialization in Section 7). Nevertheless, regardless of the normativeness of physical punishment, greater use of this form of power assertion is associated with more externalizing and internalizing problems (Lansford et al., 2005). And, in a meta-analysis that included seventy-five studies, many of them longitudinal in nature, Gershoff and Grogan-Kaylor (2016) found considerable support for the position that physical punishment leads to externalizing problems in children.

With respect to other forms of power assertion, Gershoff et al. (2010), in a study involving six different countries, found that parental yelling, scolding, and the expression of disappointment were associated with higher levels of child aggression. Time-out, teaching about good and bad behavior, encouraging children to apologize, taking away privileges, shaming, withdrawing love, threatening punishment, and promising treats and privileges did not predict aggression. The way in which these forms of power assertion are employed is important, however. For example, time-out is a favored approach to discipline that has recently been the object of concern. Dadds and Tully (2019) noted some important ways it needs to be administered so that it is not ineffective or even harmful. Accordingly, time-out, among other features, should not threaten a child's feelings of security or signal rejection, should be accompanied by reasoning and explanation, should be ended when the recipient shows evidence of self-regulation, and should involve discussion about more appropriate ways of behaving.

Withdrawal of Love.   Self-determination theorists have addressed withdrawal of love in the form of conditional negative regard or withdrawing attention and affection. Research findings indicate that this form of socialization is associated with resentment toward socializing agents, problems in emotion control, and reduced interest in the activity involved (Roth et al., 2009).

Reasoning.   Another amorphous category, along with power assertion, is reasoning, with examples including normative statements, discussion of consequences, reference to the feelings of others, and general information. The evidence continues to suggest that reasoning, and particularly reasoning that focuses on the impact of one's behavior on others, is effective in promoting positive social behavior. For example, children who were asked to work rather than play with attractive toys worked harder and longer when not under surveillance if they were told the experimenter might suffer negative consequences than if they were told they themselves would suffer negative consequences or if they were simply told to work rather than play (Kuczynski, 1983). And children were more responsive when they were told that sharing would make the recipient happy rather than when they were provided with a normative statement such as "it is good to share" (Eisenberg-Berg & Geisheker, 1979). Presumably, reasoning that focuses on the negative impact of antisocial behavior on others is more effective than other forms of reasoning because it arouses empathy for the person who has been harmed (Eisenberg et al., 2015; Hoffman, 1970). When a child's attention is focused on disappointment involving the self rather than on harm done to others, internalization of a particular value is discouraged (Ryan & Deci, 2017).

Reasoning has other features that make it more or less effective. It must, of course, be age appropriate and easily understood, as well as involving an argument seen as appropriate. It needs to be fitted to the domain of the misdeed: what works for moral transgressions or harm to others does not work for social conventional transgressions, which are not inherently bad or immoral. Children rate teachers less highly when, for example, the teacher refers to rules in the case of stealing or when the teacher talks about taking the other person's point of view in the case of swearing (Killen, 1991; Nucci, 1984).

What is Control in the Discipline Process?   "Control" associated with discipline is, in fact, a confusing concept. This is due in part, at least, to the fact that control has both positive and negative meanings. The question for researchers is how control can be applied so as to facilitate positive socialization outcomes. Baumrind (2012) addressed the issue by making a distinction between authoritative and authoritarian parenting in the forms of control they require. Equating control and power assertion, she argued that there is a difference between confrontive control, which is associated with authoritative parenting, and coercive control, which is associated with authoritarian parenting. The former includes unambivalent exercise of influence, free use of negative sanctions, and discouragement of defiance on the child's part; the latter includes arbitrary discipline, verbal hostility, psychological control, and severe physical punishment. Power assertion is exercised in both forms of parenting, but in the case of authoritative parenting it is also accompanied by responsiveness to the child's wishes and needs and by explanation. In this case, then, children can choose to comply, to argue for a mutually acceptable compromise, or to pay a known price for noncompliance. In the case of coercive control, the result for children is more likely to be evasion, resentment, or withdrawal.

Another distinction in the area of control – behavioral vs. psychological – comes from the work of Barber (1996). In Barber's analysis, behavioral control refers to setting reasonable rules for behavior and enforcement of those rules. When this manifestation of control is too great, it is associated with maladjustment; when it is too little, it is associated with antisocial behavior (Barber & Harmon, 2002). Behavioral control, then, appears to be a combination of autonomy support and structure, to use the terms of Ryan and Deci (2017). Psychological control is comprised of guilt induction, withdrawal of love, and intrusiveness, and is associated with internalizing problems such as anxiety, depression, low academic achievement, and low self-esteem. This form of control is also associated with relational aggression, with stronger effects appearing during adolescence when concerns with self-identity increase (Kuppens et al., 2013).

Yet another approach to control comes from Grolnick and Pomerantz (2009), who argued for control and structure as two separate and orthogonal features of discipline. Control, they suggested, refers to parenting that is characterized by pressure, intrusion, and domination. Its opposite is autonomy support, wherein children feel that compliance has been freely given. Structure is the provision of clear and consistent guidelines, expectations, and rules, and clear feedback about the consequences for antisocial behavior; its absence is lack of clear information regarding how one should behave.

Reward.   Reward for positive behavior forms the second part of the control domain. In this case, agents of socialization use their greater control over resources to encourage positive behavior. Reward is not without its dangers. Attribution and self-determination theorists, for example, note that material rewards given for an intrinsically motivated activity (actions that are inherently pleasurable) undermine that intrinsic motivation. Thus, children given or promised rewards for something they like to do may later spend less time at that activity than they did previously (e.g., Lepper et al., 1973). Even toddlers who are given a reward for sharing subsequently share less (Warneken & Tomasello, 2008).

The Impact of Social Rewards in Different Situations.   Rewards in the form of praise for positive social behavior that is not intrinsically motivated can be effective if they occur under certain conditions. Dweck (1975) has shown that children who are praised for their efforts in an achievement situation do better when faced with a challenge than do those who are praised for native abilities or dispositions. This is because efforts can be modified whereas native abilities cannot. Moreover, praise for inborn abilities reduces motivation to take on more challenging tasks and can lead to helpless reactions in response to failure, whereas praise for effort does not, with the latter producing "mastery-oriented" individuals.

In contrast to achievement situations, praise that focuses on the child's dispositional features has more positive effects in the case of prosocial behavior than praise for prosocial action. For example, children praised for sharing were subsequently not as likely to share as children who were told they were helpful people (Grusec & Redler, 1980). Children told either that they could help when help was needed or that they could be helpers when help was needed differed in their subsequent assistance to another individual, with the latter helping more than the former (Bryan et al., 2014). One explanation for these findings is that attributions of prosocial actions to a disposition or to a personality feature – produced either by the self or by someone else – leads to a change in self-perception and that the children in these studies, to maintain cognitive consistency, were behaving in accord with this self-perception.

Conditional Positive Regard.   Conditional positive regard, or making increases in the usual level of positive regard contingent on performance, is another form of reward that has a harmful impact. When agents of socialization make their approval contingent on the display of desired behavior the outcomes are feelings of internal compulsion, problems in emotion control, and reduced enjoyment of the activity involved (Roth et al., 2009). These outcomes overlap with the outcomes of conditional negative regard.

Praise as Encouragement.   Although praise is usually treated as reinforcement of the behavior it follows, increasing the probability that the behavior will occur in the future, it can also be seen as a way of scaffolding the learning of behavior (Dahl et al., 2017). In the latter case, praise and the encouragement that accompanies it should have a facilitative effect on behavior at the beginning stages of learning and be unnecessary at the later stages when the behavior has been internalized. In support of this analysis, Dahl and colleagues found that younger toddlers (13–15 months), who were not yet proficient at helping and who were told that they should help another adult and then praised ("You're such a great helper") more than doubled their helping compared to a control group who received no such encouragement or praise. Notably, the increase in prosocial behavior occurred in the absence of the experimenter, and therefore was unlikely to have been motivated by a desire for further approval. In contrast, older infants (15–18 months), who were more experienced helpers, did not show any increase in their helping behavior after receiving the same intervention, likely because they no longer needed such scaffolding. This discussion of praise as a way of scaffolding new learning leads to the next domain.

4.2.2 Guided Learning

In this domain, socialization agents are teachers and children are students. Because humans are less strong physically than many other species, survival skills need to be taught. Moreover, children's relatively prolonged period of dependency gives time for this learning to occur (see our earlier discussion in Section 1.1.1). Particularly pertinent for an analysis of socialization are parent–child conversations about events that are relevant to understanding and internalizing societal requirements and values. At an early age, children address a wide variety of issues in conversations with parents and others. These include other family members, illness, death, questions about fairness and moral choice, and what other people do for a living (Dunn & Hughes, 2014). Their conversations become increasingly sophisticated as, with the help of conversational partners, they coconstruct and eventually internalize rules and expectations. Through scaffolding that includes clarifying questions and reflections on, and extensions of, children's comments, social knowledge is advanced (O'Neal & Plumert, 2014). In addition to conversation, guided learning occurs when books are read to children. When the reader elicits discussion of the content, and there is an exchange of information, values are learned and knowledge regarding the emotions and social situations addressed in the book is acquired (Brownell et al., 2013; Grazzani et al., 2016). Scaffolding or guided learning can also occur when it is used to teach behavior, such as how to help, how to be polite, how to handle social interactions in a successful way, and so on. Hammond and Carpendale (2015), for example, observed mothers attempting to get their children to clean up after a tea party. Mothers who integrated their children's interests into the cleanup were more successful than those who were less attuned to their children's current focus.

Reminiscing about past experiences is another excellent opportunity for guided learning. This includes talking about times when the child was well behaved, was not well behaved, or was experiencing a positive or negative emotion, although it should be noted that Western European mothers are less likely to talk about their children's past bad behavior than are Chinese mothers (Miller et al., 2012). Learning by reminiscing is efficient because it occurs in a context where emotions are not running high and so more attention is available to listen to the message. Again, the way in which reminiscing is conducted makes a difference, with some mothers simply repeating questions and not providing a strong sense of narrative and others elaborating, asking questions, and waiting for answers. The latter are more likely to have children who exhibit emotion understanding and conscience development than the former (Laible, 2011). Moreover, reminiscing about one's past facilitates the development of a sense of self-identity or a life narrative (Laible & Panfile, 2014); children come to see themselves as helpful, kind, fair, intelligent, creative, or whatever as a result of talking about their past behavior.

4.2.3 Group Participation

In this domain, agents of socialization are members of the same social group as the child. They provide examples of behavior that are modeled or imitated by the child, as well as opportunities to partake in group customs. From an evolutionary perspective, motivation for being like others has emerged from the fact that others have to be relied on for assistance and for resources. As groups grew larger it became necessary to mark their boundaries and so symbols that distinguish the in-group from the out-group became important. These symbols have come to be seen not just as different but as better (Brewer, 1999).

Common ways of facilitating approved behavior in this domain include encouraging children's participation in desired routine activities. Children involved in prosocial activities, for example, begin to engage in those activities without great thought. In one study, children who helped with work around the home were also more likely to be helpful in other contexts, but only when work at home was done on a routine basis rather than in response to a request, and when it involved tasks that benefited other members of the family rather than just the self (Grusec et al.,1996). Cross-cultural work likewise indicates that conveying to children a sense of shared communal responsibility for family chores and work leads to much greater voluntary participation in such activities, compared to when they are assigned responsibility for specific chores or for their own care (Coppens et al., 2016).

Theories addressed to family rituals and routines highlight the meaning that is conveyed during such interactions (Fiese et al., 2002). Family rituals include celebrations, traditions, and everyday patterned routines, such as dinnertime or bedtime. They reflect – often implicitly, but pervasively – the identity, values, and culture of the family ("this is who we are"). Rituals involved in interactions with groups outside the home, such as sports teams or youth groups, create a sense of social belonging to these groups, making children more likely to adopt the behaviors and attitudes customary in them. Rituals also involve repetition, which leads to the formation of habits. Thus, simply by being exposed to group customs and routine activities, either as active participants or as observers with intent to participate in the future (Rogoff et al., 2003), children readily adopt a host of norms and expectations regarding their social world, including how to greet others, eat, dress, play, speak to elders, and act in accord with their gender.

In addition to directly participating in social rituals, or observing them first hand, children are exposed to models of behavior from their extended culture through the media they consume. Much research has focused on the effects of media models on children's social behavior. Initial studies were conducted by Bandura and his colleagues (Bandura et al., 1963), who investigated the effects of watching an adult behave in an aggressive fashion toward an inflated doll. A great many studies, as well as meta-analyses, conducted since then have, in their totality, indicated that watching aggressive models on television and in the movies, as well as playing violent video games, encourages children to behave in antisocial ways and discourages empathy and prosocial behavior (Prot et al., 2015). Other forms of undesirable behavior are likewise associated with exposure to media, such as alcohol consumption and binge drinking, sexual aggression, and gender-stereotypic attitudes and actions (Grusec, 2019). Attention has also been paid to the depiction of prosocial behavior in the media. Research indicates that this depiction has positive effects on children, including the promotion of higher levels of empathy and prosocial behavior, and lower levels of aggression (Coyne et al., 2017).

Several techniques exist to counter the negative impact of the media as well as other models of problematic behavior (Goodnow, 1997). Parents, for example, try to display positive behaviors and refrain from negative ones. They attempt to guide their children's choice of friends. They cocoon their children, keeping them away from undesirable models: cocooning is a strategy that obviously works less well as children grow older. Another strategy is pre-arming or providing ways to deal with undesirable behavior to which children might be exposed in the future. In a meta-analysis, Collier et al. (2016) compared different ways parents attempt to reduce the undesirable effects of exposure to aggressive and mature content in the media. Their analysis indicated that cocooning and setting limits on time spent in undesirable media activities, as well as setting limits on content, were effective in reducing aggression, substance abuse, and undesirable sexual behavior. Pre-arming was also associated with positive outcomes. Coviewing, either intentional or passive, was a positive predictor of antisocial behavior.

4.3 Conclusion

We have attempted to show how current conceptualizations of socialization have emerged from basic theories that dominated developmental science for many years. Although at first glance the different theories appear to offer inconsistent recommendations for effective socialization of children, we argue that these multiple viewpoints need not be seen as contradictory. Rather, they point to the importance of an approach that requires knowing which domain a child is in and, therefore, what sort of response is needed. When children are distressed they need protection, which forms a base on which to build the teaching of values. When reasonable requests are complied with, a generally cooperative relationship forms another base for successful socialization. In the context of these relationships, further teaching of values can occur when a child has behaved in an antisocial manner and needs redirection, when an opportunity for discussion presents itself, or when exposure to desirable social customs and models is available.

5 Parenting Cognitions

Parents' beliefs about events that occur during socialization – why a child behaved in a particular way, how much control each member of the dyad had over the interaction, what is acceptable behavior in a particular situation – all have an impact on their actions and, accordingly, on the success or failure of their socialization attempts (see Holden & Smith, 2019, for a summary of relevant research on this topic). We present a sample of these cognitions about parenting and the nature of their impact on the socialization process.

5.1 Parenting Self-Efficacy

Parents differ in beliefs about their ability to influence their children's behavior. These beliefs, in turn, affect their socialization practices, with self-efficacious beliefs more likely to promote positive outcomes in children. As one example, Bugental and her colleagues (Bugental & Corpuz, 2019) studied mothers who believe that their children are more influential than they themselves are when interactions are not going well. A mother who is high in perceived control over failure attributes problems to her own efforts, whereas one who is low in perceived control over failure attributes that failure to some feature of the child. The latter mothers are threatened and, depending on the situation, become either abusive and hostile or submissive in their interactions with their children. They send confusing messages to their children and so their children stop paying attention to them. Ultimately, the negative view of the power relationship impairs mothers' ability to problem solve and to be effective in the parenting role. Depression, coldness, and disengagement from the child are further outcomes.

In an intervention project, Bugental and colleagues (Bugental et al., 2002, 2012) identified mothers who were at risk for abusive parenting. These mothers were assigned to one of three conditions: a reframing condition, a standard program used for mothers at risk of abuse, and no intervention. In the first condition, mothers were helped to find benign explanations for their babies' challenging behavior. A mother who complained that her infant cried constantly because the baby was mad at her, for example, would be asked to think about what else might be causing the crying. When the mother produced a more benign explanation, such as colic, she was asked to think about ways of reducing the crying problem with assistance, if needed, from published child-care information. Mothers in the reframing condition were less likely than in the other two conditions to abuse their child and spent more time in child care. Also, their children were less aggressive at 3 years of age.

Other research coming from the perspective of Bandura's (1977) self-efficacy theory has also indicated the importance of self-efficacy for children's socialization experiences. Thus, parents' beliefs that they have a positive influence on their children has been related to a variety of positive socialization outcomes, including social competence, academic achievement, and fewer internalizing and external-izing problems (Glatz & Buchanan, 2015; Jones & Prinz, 2005).

5.2 Attributions

Research on self-efficacy focuses on the role of perceptions of one's own ability and its impact on parenting. Additionally, however, parents look for explanations for the actions of their children – explanations that also have an impact on the parenting process. When children misbehave, for example, that behavior can be attributed to the child's character (a dispositional or internal attribution) or to features of the situation (a situational or external attribution). When parents make dispositional attributions for bad behavior, and when they see that behavior as intentional or under the child's control, then they are likely to experience negative affect. They are also more likely to be punitive, a particularly harmful reaction if the child's action was indeed not intentional. Mothers who make negative attributions are more likely to have children who are aggressive, hyperactive, socially withdrawn, or conduct-disordered, presumably a reflection of ineffective parenting practices (Grusec et al., 1997).

5.3 Goals

Goals are different from values, with the latter involving strongly held beliefs that parents try to instill in their children. Goals, by contrast, refer to the parents' desired outcome in a given parenting intervention. Hastings and Grusec (1998), for example, interviewed parents about a recent time when their child had misbehaved and asked them to describe the event as well as what their goal was in the interaction. Three goals were identified, with these goals being either short term or long term. They were: parent-centered – wanting the child to obey in the present (short-term) and to be obedient and respectful in the future (long-term); child-centered – wanting to understand the child's point of view at the moment (short-term) and wanting the child to acquire a particular value to guide future action (long-term); and relationship-centered – wanting to reach a happy and fair resolution (short-term) and to build love, trust, and close family connections (long-term). Not surprisingly, parent-centered goals were linked to the use of power assertion, child-centered ones to reasoning, and relationship-centered goals to warmth and negotiation. Additionally, Hastings and Grusec found that women were more likely than men to focus on relationship-centered goals.

5.4 Mindfulness

Mindfulness is the ability to be aware of and to regulate one's emotional experience, and to attend to one's surroundings and situational cues in the present moment, rather than to be immersed in past happenings or expectations related to future events. Research relating mindfulness to parenting indicates that mindful parents are higher in authoritative beliefs and lower in authoritarian ones (Williams & Wahler, 2010). Mindful parents also exhibit lower levels of stress (e.g., Gouveia et al., 2016). Kil and Grusec (2020) found that mothers' dispositional mindfulness predicted less maternal stress, which in turn mediated the link to young adolescents' reports that their mothers took their perspective and understood them. Furthermore, they found that mothers' greater mindfulness was associated with adolescents' willingness to disclose information to their mothers, as well as the adolescents' ratings of less intense disagreements with their mothers: these relations were mediated by maternal stress and perceptions of maternal perspective-taking.

6 Siblings and Peers as Agents of Socialization

Parents are the primary agents of socialization for the many reasons cited in Section 1.1. Nevertheless, there are other individuals who have an impact on children's learning of values and socially acceptable behavior. These include siblings, peers, teachers, coaches, grandparents, and other members of the child's extended family. We elaborate upon the roles of siblings and peers, because their influences on socialization are quite different from those of parents (or other adults), yet still very important.

6.1 Siblings as Agents of Socialization

Siblings spend considerable time in each other's company and are, in fact, each other's most constant companions outside the school setting. Sibling relationships differ from, but also have features in common with, parent–child relationships: they are not voluntary, a feature meaning that extra effort needs to be expended in creating harmonious interactions. Siblings can also be involved in caregiving to varying degrees across cultures, with parents temporarily, or even on a more extensive basis, transferring their authority and supervisory responsibilities to an older child (Kramer & Hamilton, 2019).

One of the key features of sibling relationships is their emotional intensity, both negative and positive (Dunn, 2015). The negative interactions can manifest themselves in conflict and aggressive behaviors: the most common form of domestic abuse, for example, is sibling violence (Naylor et al., 2011). Sustained and increasing antisocial behavior on the part of siblings has been shown to predict bullying, refusal to share with unfamiliar peers, and social exclusion (Ensor et al., 2010). However, siblings can also be important sources of comfort and caring: children growing up in homes characterized by harshness, for example, have fewer adjustment problems if they have a good sibling relationship (Jenkins, 1992).

6.1.1 Protection

Because of the amount of time they spend together, as well as the intensity of the emotional experiences they share, siblings are in a position to provide support for each other in response to stressful experiences, with this provision of comfort and help increasing with age (Abramovitch et al., 1986). Siblings report greater closeness and intimacy when there is a death or divorce in the family, maternal illness, or personal accidents and illnesses, as well as conflicts with other children (Dunn et al., 1994). Another example of how sibling relationships provide a protective function comes from a longitudinal study showing that sibling support reduces the negative effect of parental hostility on sisters' observed hostility in their own romantic relationships (although not in the case of brothers; Masarik & Rogers, 2019). It should be noted that sibling influences are bidirectional, with younger and older siblings affecting each other. In a longitudinal study, for example, Jambon et al., (2019) assessed the development of empathic concern in younger (toddler) and older (preschool) children at two points in time approximately 18 months apart. They found that both younger and older siblings contributed to the development of their sibling's empathic concern between the two time points. Moreover, the effects were obtained when parenting practices and demographic variables were controlled for. In addition to evidence for the impact of each sibling on the other's empathy, the results of this investigation also yielded a stronger effect for the influence of older siblings in dyads that were further apart in age.

6.1.2 Reciprocity

Siblings play together, and in the course of that play they learn social skills, including how to cooperate with others and to appreciate their perspective (Dunn, 2015). Thus, younger siblings who report reciprocal interactions (mutual and egalitarian exchanges) with their older siblings are more likely to have good socioemotional problem-solving skills. In contrast, interactions between siblings involving assistance and instruction are not associated with social skills (Karos et al., 2007). Comparisons between children with and without siblings showed that social competence with peers was greater in those children with siblings. Although the quality of individual peer relationships did not differ between singletons and children with siblings, singletons were less liked overall by classmates. As well, singletons were more likely to be victimized and more likely to be aggressive toward their peers (Kitzmann et al., 2002).

6.1.3 Control

A major experience for siblings in the control domain is learning how to resolve conflicts. In these situations, siblings try to obtain their goals either with aggression or with negotiation (Zukow-Goldring, 2002). The negative outcomes of aggression as a form of conflict resolution are clear in the work of Patterson and his colleagues, who observed how siblings reinforce each other's aggression by fighting back. When siblings train each other to be coercive, not only do they reinforce undesirable behavior, they also fail to encourage prosocial behavior, including social understanding and emotion regulation, as well as empathy (Snyder & Patterson, 1995). When these positive skills are lacking, hostility in the sibling relationship increases. Although physically aggressive behavior declines as siblings move into middle childhood, other forms of aggression – verbal and relational – remain. A more positive approach to conflict resolution involves negotiation. Here, siblings learn the importance of modifying their own behavior in accord with the needs of their partner. Through conflict, then, siblings can learn social problem-solving strategies and the importance of mutual consensus (Recchia & Howe, 2009).

6.1.4 Guided Learning

Siblings are particularly suited to teaching social cognitive skills to their younger siblings because they are closer to their zone of proximal development and therefore may find it easier to understand their point of view and guide their learning (Cassidy et al., 2005). Sibling teaching is also influenced by the age and gender of both siblings, with older sisters teaching more than older brothers and younger sisters eliciting more teaching than younger brothers (Azmitia & Hesser, 1993; Stoneman et al., 1986). The amount of teaching by siblings also increases with age (Mendelson & Gottlieb, 1994), including teaching that is related to feelings and emotions (Brown & Dunn, 1992). Thus, middle childhood is a particularly important time for guided learning or instruction within sibling relationships.

Some evidence comparing siblings and peers as teachers suggests that siblings are more effective at teaching than peers. Azmitia and Hesser (1993), for example, observed that younger siblings resisted the attempts of older siblings to take over a task to a greater extent than was the case with peers: this finding suggests an increased need for personal responsibility and assertive abilities with siblings than with peers. Children in this study also requested more help, asked more questions, and challenged their siblings more than was the case with peers. Maccoby (1984) noted that sibling teaching interactions become more coregulated during middle childhood, with this increase in input from younger siblings also resulting in better learning than with peers.

Teaching interactions can benefit the older sibling as well. Scaffolding requires understanding of the other's mind, tailoring one's explanation accordingly, and articulating that explanation clearly. Practicing these skills with younger siblings can lead to cognitive growth. Accordingly, Smith (1993) found that adolescents who reported more academic teaching of their younger siblings showed a greater increase in their verbal abilities (assessed using standardized tests) over a two-year period.

6.1.5 Group Participation

Older siblings provide multiple opportunities for their younger siblings to learn through observing their behavior, and thereby to gain knowledge about the ways of thinking and acting in their social groups. One example is the socialization of gender. Children with older brothers are more likely to engage in masculine play activities and, contrarily, children with older sisters in feminine play activities (Stoneman et al., 1986). Sometimes the effect can be in the opposite direction, with older girls less feminine when they have younger brothers (McHale et al., 2001). Older siblings can also act as negative role models, as well as introduce their younger siblings to antisocial peers (Bank et al., 1996). The effect is particularly strong with male siblings who are close in age and who therefore presumably spend more time together (Rowe et al., 1992). The effects of frequency of interaction are apparent in the finding that time spent together is a mediator of the relation between genetic similarity and risky attitudes to sexual behavior (McHale et al., 2009). Another socialization outcome linked to sibling behavior is academic achievement. Thus, Wang et al. (2019) found that older siblings whose peers were academically disengaged (who found school a waste of time) in Grade 7 were more likely, two years later, to have younger siblings whose interactions with academically disengaged peers increased, while those with academically engaged peers decreased.

Older siblings are an excellent source of information about appropriate social behavior and, therefore, highly likely to have their actions imitated, albeit with the kinds of exceptions noted earlier. The phenomenon of "de-identification," however, also occurs when children behave in a way that is opposite to that of a sibling. Such behavior enables children to set themselves apart as unique members of the family, as well as reducing sibling rivalry. Most second-born siblings report wanting to be like an older sibling, although also wanting to compete in at least some areas (Whiteman et al., 2007). Whiteman et al. found a second group of siblings, however, who wanted to be different and not to compete. A third group did not use their older siblings as referents for either modeling or deidentification. It would seem, then, that the special features of the sibling relationship – having to live together and share the attention of the same adults – can sometimes work against the desire to be like other members of the social group.

6.2 Peers as Agents of Socialization

Children can spend more time with peers, beginning in day care, than they do with siblings. Peers become even more important in the socialization process as middle childhood is reached and a primary concern becomes being liked by one's peers, belonging to a group, and developing deep emotional bonds with friends. A marked difference between parents, siblings, and peers, of course, is that peers need not maintain an unsatisfactory relationship whereas parents and siblings must do so. Thus, pressures to interact and cooperate are greater for family members than they are for peers.

6.2.1 Protection

Children turn to their friends when they are distressed, and these peers, in turn, act as emotion regulation coaches. As of early adolescence, friends are seen to be just as supportive as parents, or even more so (Bokhorst et al., 2010). There are gender differences in how boys and girls function with their peers in the protection domain: both boys and girls seek peer support when they are stressed, but girls are more likely than boys to do so (Rose et al., 2012). Klimes-Dougan et al. (2013) assessed different expectations boys and girls had for how their distress would be received by peers. They found that friends were perceived to respond to distress by providing comfort and acceptance or by dismissing or minimizing the value of the emotion, rather than with punitive reactions; however, girls reported higher levels of positive responses than boys, who reported that their friends were more likely to use overt and relational aggression as well as to ignore the emotional response. This finding no doubt reflects the greater tendency of girls to talk about emotions (Chaparro & Grusec, 2016).

One important area for comfort and support, not surprisingly, is bullying: the frequency of comfort-seeking in this particular situation also increases with age (Hunter et al., 2004). Additionally, having a friend who "sticks up" for them means that children who are bullied are less likely to exhibit increases in internalizing or externalizing behavior that would otherwise occur (Hodges et al., 1999).

Are some children better at providing comfort than others? Children are more likely to be helpful and kind to peers when they themselves display lower levels of negative emotions in the classroom and at home (Eisenberg et al., 1996), presumably because their better emotion control frees them to recognize and to be responsive to difficulties in others. Social status is another determinant of caring behavior, with members of influential peer groups more likely to be identified by classmates as helpful and kind (Ellis & Zarbatany, 2007).

6.2.2 Reciprocity

Peer interactions in the reciprocity domain are frequent as children play together, work cooperatively, and establish friendships. The benefits of cooperative play have been demonstrated in a number of studies focused on cooperative learning environments. Participating in cooperative learning groups during the academic year increases children's liking of each other at the end of the year (Smith et al.,1993), promotes better performance on academic tasks such as problem-solving and knowledge acquisition (Johnson & Johnson, 1979), and facilitates performance when guidelines for cooperative learning are provided (Gillies & Ashman, 1998). More recent interest has turned to the effects of playing cooperative as opposed to competitive video games, with children asked, for example, to rate the frequency they play games where they have to work together with others or where they have to play against others. Lobel et al. (2017), in a longitudinal study, reported that competitive gaming was associated with decreases in prosocial behavior, but only in the case of children who played video games with high frequency.

Friendships become increasingly important as children grow older, with an emphasis on intimate and mutual relationships. Reciprocity is a significant feature of friendships and, so long as cooperation with the other's needs and requests continues, friendships endure (Hartup & Abecassis, 2002). Moreover, children who have close mutual friendships engage in more cooperative play, are more prosocial and sociable, and have fewer peer conflicts (Howe, 1989).

6.2.3 Control

Peers encourage adherence to group norms so as to maintain harmony and social status within the group. They apply pressure either through positive reactions, such as praise, or through negative ones, such as criticism and exclusion from the group (Parke et al., 2019). Other negative peer influences come in the form of peer pressure to behave in risky or antisocial ways. The important role played by this type of peer pressure in the development of antisocial behavior is highlighted in the finding that it is the strongest predictor of delinquency after early emotional and behavioral problems (Sullivan, 2006).

A not uncommon way of exerting control in peer interactions is through bullying, which often starts as a way of displaying disapproval toward a child who is different. When peers enable bullying its effects are particularly negative. For example, the links between social anxiety and peer rejection are strongest in classrooms where bullying was reinforced by classmates and victims were not likely to be defended (Kärnä et al., 2010).

6.2.4 Guided Learning

As noted in our discussion of guided learning and siblings, there is some evidence that siblings are better teachers than peers. Nevertheless, peers have a role to play in this domain. Peers, of course, are relatively similar in their levels of competence and ability, a fact that may aid them in the teaching process. In a study of the development of moral reasoning, for example, Walker et al. (2000) found that peers who talked together in a supportive way showed higher rates of development in this area than those who did not engage in such exchanges. Unlike the situation of parent as teacher, peer–peer interactions that had a negative and hostile tone were also effective in promoting moral development. This finding, presumably, can be explained by the greater ability of peers to tolerate conflict because of their more egalitarian relationship. Finally, friends are more effective teachers than other peers because they share more information about the task at hand and contribute more elaborated ideas (MacDonald et al., 2002).

6.2.5 Group Participation

Forming groups and cliques, and becoming similar in areas such as clothing, music, and food habits, is an important part of middle childhood and adolescence (Parke et al., 2019). Here, modeling of others' behavior, as well as adjusting one's own actions through comparison with others, are central (Harter, 2006; Lubbers et al., 2009). Similarity between group members can be the outcome of seeking out or being attracted to those whom one resembles ("homophily") or, in the case of group participation, taking on the characteristics of others through association and lengthy exposure. No doubt both are in operation.

Belonging to a group is necessary for general adjustment, although if the values of the group involve antisocial actions such as delinquency, substance use, and reduced achievement aspirations, then adjustment will obviously be negatively affected (Lubbers et al., 2009). An example of how parents may affect the peer groups their children choose to join was provided by Durbin et al. (1993). They found that children who categorized their parents as authoritative were attracted to well-rounded crowds with positive values, whereas those with uninvolved parents (low on both support and limit setting) tended to join groups with antisocial values ("druggies" and "partyers"). Boys with indulgent parents were attracted to crowds with a "fun-culture" orientation.

7 Cultural Influences on Socialization

The broad social context within which the child functions plays a crucial role in the socialization process. Bronfenbrenner (1977) proposed an important model that outlines the different influences on the developing child. In addition to the child's biology and to the immediate settings with which the child comes into direct contact, such as the home and classroom (the "microsystem"), Bronfenbrenner identified several indirect influences. These indirect influences provide the broader social context, or social ecology, in which the child's immediate environments are embedded. They include two levels. The first is the "exosystem," which involves institutions and structures which children do not interact with directly, but which nevertheless affect them by influencing their socialization agents (e.g., the parents' work environment, the school board, services in the community for parents). The second and broadest sphere is the culture or "macrosystem." This system includes the norms, values, customs, expectations, and beliefs that tend to be shared by people of the same social group. Culture, because it provides the widest context within which socialization occurs, can have profound implications both in terms of content – what children learn about ways of thinking and doing things in the world, and in terms of process – how children come to learn these lessons.

The influence of culture, however, is qualified in two important ways. First, there is a great deal of variability in values, attitudes, and behaviors not only between cultures but also within cultures (Lansford et al., 2018). Although differences between cultures can be important, the intracultural variations (the differences between families from the same culture) are just as meaningful for understanding a child's socialization and development. Second, despite important differences between cultures, there are also processes that are similar across cultures. For example, humans have biologically based behavioral tendencies which have evolved because they helped solve recurrent problems encountered by our ancestors, and many of these universal tendencies are relevant to childrearing and socialization (see Section 1.1.1). Nowadays as well, parents across many cultures have common goals and challenges, such as keeping their children healthy and safe, and promoting their development, education, and positive adjustment (Bornstein & Lansford, 2019). The five domains of socialization that we have outlined in this Element (see Sections 4 and 6) also refer to basic human experiences (being protected, being reciprocated, being in conflict, being guided, and being part of a group); although cultures can differ in their expectations and customs regarding each of these situations, the experiences themselves are a fundamental part of being human.

Nevertheless, the remainder of this section will focus on differences between cultures. We focus on two types of differences: mean differences between cultures (main effects) and differences in the links between caregiving behaviors and child outcomes as a function of culture (culture as a moderator).

7.1 Mean Differences Between Cultures in Socialization Practices

Children growing up in different cultures can have vastly different socialization experiences. These can range from who takes care of children, who lives in the family home, and where children sleep; through how children are played with, talked to, or how and when they are disciplined; to how much autonomy they are given, the nature of their leisure activities, their responsibilities, and what skills they are taught. All can vary as a function of the cultural context, with mean differences in these and many other aspects of socialization observed between different cultures (e.g., Harkness & Super, 2002; Super & Harkness, 2002).

In each of the five domains of socialization, children's experiences differ across cultures. In the protection domain, for example, cultural messages regarding independence and the need to soothe one's self versus dependency on the caregiver for soothing are conveyed through whether infants and young children sleep in a separate bed and/or room, as is typical in Western cultures, or cosleep with parents or siblings (Morelli et al., 1992; Owens, 2004). Face-to-face play interactions, which afford opportunities for reciprocity in infancy and toddler-hood, also differ as a function of culture. The frequency of such interactions varies considerably by culture, as does the identity of the partners involved (for example, whether such reciprocity is experienced with parents, or primarily with siblings rather than with adults; Bornstein et al., 2006). Mothers also talk to their children differently in different cultures. European American mothers, for example, use greater labeling of objects, whereas Japanese mothers are more likely to engage children in social rituals ("I give it to you. Now you give it to me. Thank you!"; Fernald & Morikawa, 1993, p. 653). In this example, mothers from these two cultures use guided learning interactions to teach different skills, which correspond to cultural differences in values and expectations. Thus, there is a greater focus of European American mothers on children's verbal maturity and mastery of the external environment compared to Japanese mothers' greater emphasis on emotional maturity and social courtesy (Bornstein & Lansford, 2019). Cultures also differ in parenting practices in the control domain. For example, the frequency of using corporal punishment and endorsing its use as necessary for successful childrearing varies greatly among countries (Bornstein & Lansford, 2019; Lansford et al., 2005). Experiences in the group participation domain are also vastly different. For example, in cultures where children attend school there is relatively little access to adult activities and the focus is on separate tasks such as learning and play. In contrast, in indigenous cultures, children are integrated into the same "adult" family and community activities, and therefore learn to collaborate, share responsibility, and contribute to these endeavors on their own initiative (Coppens et al., 2016).

7.2 Culture as Moderator of the Associations Between Socialization Practices and Child Outcomes

In addition to mean differences in caregiving practices between cultures, some associations between caregiving practices and child outcomes also vary from one culture to another. Thus, the relation between a parenting variable and a child outcome may be positive in one cultural context yet substantially weaker, nonexistent, or even negative in a different cultural context. These effects have been most frequently examined regarding parenting behaviors in the control domain, although they can also occur with a wide range of other parenting behaviors (Lansford et al., 2018). For example, as noted in Section 4.2.1, the link between parental use of corporal punishment and children's behavior problems is much stronger in families of European American background compared to African American families (Deater-Deckard et al., 1996;

Lansford et al., 2004), and likewise stronger in countries where corporal punishment is used infrequently and seen as non-normative compared to cultures where it is widely used and accepted (Lansford et al., 2005). Similarly, more authoritative and less authoritarian parenting has been linked to European American adolescents' positive academic functioning and greater sense of closeness to parents, yet these associations were not seen among Chinese American adolescents (Chao, 2001). Culture has also been shown to moderate the links between parental psychological control and children's psychological functioning. For example, mothers' use of guilt induction, shaming, and love withdrawal when their children misbehaved in the academic domain (e.g., did not do homework) was not associated with children's internalizing difficulties in Israeli-origin families, but was linked to fewer internalizing difficulties in families in which the parents had immigrated to Israel from the Former Soviet Union (FSU), a social group which places a particularly high value on academic achievement (Davidov & Atzaba-Poria, 2016).

How does culture act as a moderator? The ability of the cultural context to modify the association between a parenting variable and a child outcome likely lies in the different meaning that the same behavior can have in different cultures (see, for example, Section 4.2.1; Bornstein, 2009). Due to cultural differences in values, norms, and expectations, a given parenting behavior (for example, punitive discipline) can typically stem from a particular motivation in one culture (for example, hostility toward the child), yet from a very different motivation in another culture (such as a desire to instill an important message in a culturally acceptable way). Given the different meanings of the same behavior in the two cultures, it is more likely that punitive discipline will be associated with negative child outcomes when it has hostile connotations, but less likely when it is intended as part of a teaching undertaking. As an example, authoritarian/controlling parenting has been associated with more negative parenting cognitions and reduced warmth toward the child in Anglo Canadian parents, but not in parents who emigrated from Middle Eastern countries, suggesting that this form of parenting has a more negative meaning in the former cultural group (Rudy & Grusec, 2001, 2006). Moreover, perceptions by parents and children that the parenting practice is normative within their culture acts as a moderator, typically reducing the negative consequences or increasing the positive consequences of the parenting behavior (Gershoff et al., 2010; Lansford et al., 2005, 2018). Normative practices are likely typically experienced as less harmful or more supportive, with this more benign or positive meaning of the behavior serving to ameliorate its impact on the child.

In summary, research on the macrosystem reveals the considerable impact of culture on socialization. This impact is revealed both in mean-level differences between cultures in caregiving practices across all five domains and in the differential effects of the same caregiving practice on children as a function of the cultural setting to which the child and caregiver belong (at present studied primarily in the control domain). Together with these cultural differences, of course, research also reveals important within-culture variability, as well as some similarities between cultures reflecting more universal processes. All these different influences are important for a comprehensive understanding of the socialization process.

8 Biological Aspects of Socialization

Socialization is deeply rooted in our biology. In this section we discuss how the brain and hormones are implicated in socialization, as well as the roles played by genes.

8.1 Brain Functioning and Socialization

The majority of the work on brain processes involved in socialization has focused on infancy, particularly on mother–infant interactions, although studies of fathers' and nonparents' reactions to infants also exist (Frenkel & Fox, 2015). From birth, human infants and adults are predisposed to attend to each other's cues. This mutual "orienting system" (Parsons et al., 2010; Stark et al., 2019) ensures that infants and caregivers stay in close proximity to and interact with each other, a prerequisite for survival and for socialization in the protection and reciprocity domains. Accordingly, infants are drawn to social stimuli, such as human faces and speech, over nonsocial stimuli. For example, they prefer images of faces over images that contain the same features as a face but are organized in a different, nonface-like manner, and they prefer speech sounds over sounds that have similar qualities to human speech, such as pitch and volume, but are nonspeech sounds (Parsons et al., 2010). With repeated exposure, infants begin to recognize, discriminate, and prefer the face, voice, and other physical characteristics of their caregivers (Frenkel & Fox, 2015). This preference for caregivers reflects the formation of attachment and reciprocity relationships, and makes sense from an evolutionary point of view, because caregivers are the people children can rely on most for protection and support, as well as from whom they can expect reciprocal positive exchanges.

Likewise, adults are attracted to and responsive to infant characteristics and signals, both positive infant stimuli, such as pictures of infants' faces or recordings of infants' cooing or babbling sounds, and negative infant stimuli, such as crying. With respect to positive infant information, infants' characteristically appealing features, such as large eyes, large forehead, chubby cheeks,

and small chin, as well as their pleasant sounds and smells, are highly attractive to adults, including both men and women and parents and nonparents
(Kringelbach et al., 2016). This conclusion is reflected, for example, in higher
ratings of attractiveness of faces with infantile ("cuteness") features, greater
exertion of effort to view such faces, and greater activation of key brain areas
in response to such faces (Kringelbach et al., 2016; Parsons et al., 2013).
Adults are not only drawn to infants but also act intuitively to maintain and
promote engagement with them by, for example, seeking to make eye contact
and using infant-directed speech ("motherese"), which is preferred by infants
(Stark et al., 2019). The appealing features of infants therefore serve to attract
caregivers' attention, pleasure, and affection, and to sustain their engagement
and positive exchanges with infants, which are all central to the reciprocity
domain.

With respect to infants' negative cues, such as distress and crying, these are
also rapidly detected by adults and given primacy in brain processing
(Kringelbach et al., 2016; Stark et al., 2019). Infant crying is highly aversive
to adults, serving to move them to action. Indeed, across cultures, mothers
automatically respond to their infants' cries by picking them up and speaking to
them. Brain scans similarly reveal the quick activation of areas responsible for
motor action and speech in mothers upon hearing their infants' crying, compared to noncrying sounds with similar volume and pitch (Bornstein et al.,
2017). This biologically mediated response to crying is central to the protection
aspect of the parent–child relationship, as it motivates caregivers' responsiveness to distress and can thus foster the formation of a secure attachment.

The adult brain, then, is strongly responsive to positive and negative infant
stimuli, and such input is given priority in unconscious and conscious processing of information. This privileged processing includes very rapid detection of
infant signals in areas of the brainstem (Parsons et al., 2013). The information
conveyed by these signals is subsequently relayed to and processed in multiple
brain areas, including those relevant to emotion processing (amygdala and
insula), salience detection, and reward evaluation (orbitofrontal context, or
OFC), as well as areas involved in preparation for motor action (motor cortex)
and areas responsible for conscious cognitive evaluation and self-control (pre-
frontal cortex; Frenkel & Fox, 2015; Stark et al., 2019). The OFC appears to be
a central hub for the processing of infant stimuli (as well as social stimuli more
broadly). In addition to its role in detection and evaluation of rewards noted
earlier, it receives information from the five senses and interconnects with areas
responsible for emotional, motor, and cognitive processing (Kringelbach et al.,
2016; Parsons et al., 2013; Stark et al., 2019). It thus appears to play a key role in
the neural network composing the "parental brain."

With greater experience and learning, parents also show privileged processing of stimuli pertaining to their own child. For example, in an fMRI study
Bartels and Zeki (2004) found that brain activation in key areas was greater
when mothers observed photos of their own child compared to photos of another
familiar child or to those of a friend (and even compared to activation patterns
found in romantic love). One of these focal areas was the OFC, consistent with
its central role noted earlier. Longitudinal studies examining changes in parental
brain circuitry and function over time, including beyond infancy, are needed to
shed light on structural and functional changes in the OFC and other pertinent
areas as a result of parenting experience.

Socialization experiences also impact the developing child's brain in profound ways, including both the brain's structure and its function. Early work
focused on the neural correlates of extremely adverse rearing experiences,
primarily child abuse and institutionalization, as a marker of severe parental
neglect and deprivation. This work revealed reduced volume in multiple brain
regions and abnormal activation patterns compared to controls (Belsky & Haan,
2011). More recent studies have examined variations in normative parenting
behaviors and their links to individual differences in children's and adolescents'
brain structure and function. Accumulating evidence indicates that supportive
parenting practices are linked to more efficient cortical activity and to reduced
activity in regions responsible for detection of salient cues in the environment
("salience detection," for example, the amygdala). Thus, over-arousal is pre-
vented and emotion regulation and coping facilitated (Tan et al., 2020).
Moreover, negative parenting, such as controlling, critical, or intrusive parenting behavior, is associated with increased neural reactivity to negative emotional cues; such parenting has been linked to patterns of activity in key cortical
and subcortical areas and their interconnections, which have been shown to
hinder emotion regulation (Tan et al., 2020).

8.2 Hormones and Socialization

Socialization processes also involve the endocrine systems of both parent and
child. In this system, hormones transmit messages between body cells, affecting
the individual's physiology and behavior. The effects of hormones in humans
are complex, as they are modified by context, relationships, and prior experience, as well as by the interplay with genes and between different hormones
(Feldman, 2019; Flinn et al., 2005; Priel et al., 2019).

A hormone that plays a central role in parent–child relationships, and in
social bonding more broadly, is oxytocin (OT). Indeed, Carter (2014, p. 17)
concluded that "oxytocin acts to allow the high levels of social sensitivity and

attunement necessary for human sociality and for rearing a human child." Accordingly, OT appears to enhance caregivers' motivation to interact with and nurture children, thereby providing the fundamental basis for socialization. Moreover, the relation between OT and parenting behavior is bidirectional, with caregiving behavior elevating OT levels in turn. For example, OT levels in pregnancy and postpartum prime maternal caregiving behaviors toward the infant, but committed parenting behavior also elevates caregivers' OT levels as seen, for example, in fathers and adoptive parents (Feldman, 2019; Feldman & Bakermans-Kranenburg, 2017). OT is also implicated in parents' unique bond with their own child: increased activity in brain areas with a high density of OT receptors has been found when mothers observed images of their own child compared to another familiar child (Bartels & Zeki, 2004).

Levels of OT in parents affect not only the parent, but also the child. First, OT levels in the parent are correlated with, and, in fact, appear to influence, OT levels in the child (Feldman, 2019; Feldman & Bakermans-Kranenburg, 2017). For example, experimental OT administration to fathers increases the child's OT levels, with this effect mediated by increases in affectionate synchronous interaction. Additionally, postpartum depression is associated with diminished OT levels in both mother and infant. Second, children's higher levels of OT appear to increase their social attunement to caregivers, as well as to social partners more broadly, which can help facilitate socialization in important ways, such as forming relationships with others and learning from them. Thus, parent and child OT functioning, and associated patterns of synchronous parent–child behavior, have been linked to children's subsequent social competencies, including emotion regulation skills and social reciprocity with best friend (Feldman, 2019; Feldman & Bakermans-Kranenburg, 2017).

Oxytocin, then, appears to play a key role in the formation of parent–child bonds, particularly in the reciprocity domain. Other hormones are also implicated in parenting and socialization processes, including vasopressin, opioids, dopamine, testosterone, serotonin, and cortisol (Bugental, 2000; Feldman, 2019; Flinn et al., 2005). Cortisol has received considerable research attention with respect to how early socialization experiences in the protection domain influence its functioning in children.

Cortisol is secreted as part of the limbic hypothalamic–pituitary–adrenocortical (L-HPA) system. It functions to allocate and mobilize physiological resources for coping with an acute stressor (and away from maintenance and growth metabolic processes). During infancy, responsive parenting and the formation of a secure attachment are important for the adaptive regulation and long-term development of the L-HPA system, with implications for the individual's subsequent health and socioemotional competence, including the ability to cope with stressors and challenges. Appropriate parenting in the protection domain enables children to deal with everyday stressors without an accompanying increase in cortisol (Gunnar & Donzella, 2002). Children with unresponsive caregivers or insecure attachment histories show elevated cortisol levels for events such as separations and inoculations, whereas children with responsive caregivers or secure attachment do not. When caregivers are supportive, then, a cortisol response is triggered in fewer, more warranted, situations, allowing the L-HPA system to develop and function effectively. Children who have experienced chronic or severe early adversity, on the other hand, are at increased risk of developing abnormal cortisol regulation. Abnormal patterns can include either chronically high levels, or too low (blunted) levels, both of which are related to poorer ability to cope with stress (Flinn et al., 2005; Gunnar & Donzella, 2002). In addition to the protection domain, cortisol is also implicated in the control domain. Thus, conflict with parents and parental disapproval or shaming are among those events that trigger a cortisol response in children (Flinn et al., 2005).

8.3 Genetics and Socialization

Although genes contribute both to the similarities in behavioral mechanisms across all people and to individual differences in characteristics between people, genetic research pertaining to parenting and socialization invariably focuses on the latter. Thus, the primary interest of developmentalists has been on genetic contributions to variability in parenting behavior and children's socialization outcomes. This body of work has revealed several types of genetic effects, discussed below, relevant to all five domains of socialization.

8.3.1 Parents' Genes Influence Their Parenting Behavior

The impact of parents' genetic makeup on their parenting behavior is assessed through genetically informed designs such as children-of-twins studies (McAdams et al., 2014). These studies examine the level of similarity in the parenting of adult monozygotic and dizygotic twin pairs toward their respective children, in order to separate genetic and environmental effects on parenting behavior. A meta-analysis of such studies has shown moderate genetic contributions (28%–37%) to mothers' and fathers' parental warmth and negativity (relevant to the reciprocity and protection domains), but not to parental control (Klahr & Burt, 2014). Other evidence for the effects of parents' genes on their parenting behavior comes from a longitudinal molecular genetics study, which used information from parents' entire genome ("genome-wide association study"; Wertz et al., 2019). Each parent in the study received a score reflecting the quantity of genetic markers in their DNA that had been shown in prior work to predict educational attainment, an important positive adjustment outcome. This score predicted observed positive parenting behaviors pertaining to the reciprocity and protection domains (warmth, sensitivity), and to the guided learning domain (cognitive stimulation), even after controlling for the quality of caregiving that the parents received as children, and the age at which they became parents. Moreover, these genetic effects on parenting were mediated by the cognitive and self-control abilities of the parents, as assessed when they were children. In other words, parents' genes that were linked in prior work to educational attainment influenced their cognitive and self-control abilities in childhood, long before they became parents, which in turn predicted warmer, more sensitive, and more stimulating parenting behavior once they had children.

8.3.2 Children's Genes Influence the Parenting They Receive

Parents' behavior is influenced not only by their own genes, but by their children's genes as well. This effect is typically referred to as "evocative genotype-environment correlation" (Avinun & Knafo-Noam, 2015) and denotes the fact that children's genetically influenced characteristics (temperament, physical attributes, and so on) can evoke particular forms of treatment from parents and other socialization agents. Such evocative effects have been demonstrated using different types of genetically informed studies. One such design is the typical twin study, in which parents' behavior is examined toward both of their twins in monozygotic vs. dizygotic twin pairs; greater similarity in parenting toward monozygotic twins indicates that this parenting behavior is influenced by the child's genetic makeup. Such studies have shown evocative child genetic effects on the quality of parenting in multiple domains, including parental control, warmth, and negativity (Klahr & Burt, 2014), parental stress (Ayoub et al., 2019), and effective limit setting (Euser et al., 2020).

Additional evidence that children's genes influence parenting comes from adoption studies. When associations are found between adoptive parents' behavior and birth parents' characteristics, they indicate the effect of the child's genes (inherited from the birth parent) on the adoptive parents' behavior. For example, Klahr et al. (2017) found that adoptive fathers', but not mothers', less effective parenting in the control domain (negative, harsh parenting) was predicted in part by the birth parents' antisocial behavior. Similarly, Leve et al. (2019) showed that birth mothers' internalizing symptoms predicted adoptive parents' greater hostility toward the child, with this effect mediated by children's self-regulation abilities. Thus, children who were at genetic risk because their biological mothers had more internalizing symptoms showed poorer self-regulation, which in turn increased adoptive parents' ineffective responses in the control domain (hostility). An evocative effect on parental hostility has also been shown in a genome-wide association study, in which nearly 23 percent of the variability in parents' negativity was accounted for by the variation in the genetic makeup of their children (Dobewall et al., 2019).

8.3.3 Links between Parenting and Child Behavior are Partially Mediated by Shared Genes

When associations are found between parenting behaviors and child outcomes, especially longitudinal links, it is tempting to interpret them as evidence of socialization effects. However, it is important to remember that parents provide children not only with caregiving behavior, but also with their genes. Thus, links between parenting behavior and child outcomes might not reflect parenting effects but, rather, the shared genetic makeup between parent and child. If, for example, parent and child share genes supporting musicality, the parent is more likely to expose the child to musical activities (reflecting the guided leaning and group participation domains) and the child is likely to exhibit musical talents, but the underlying cause might be their similar genes rather than parental socialization. This phenomenon is referred to as "passive genotype-environment correlation" (Avinun & Knafo-Noam, 2015).

Some genetically informed studies have shown that a passive genetic effect can at least partly account for the associations between parenting and certain child outcomes (e.g., Marceau et al., 2015; Wertz et al., 2020). However, other studies have not found such effects (e.g., Hannigan et al., 2018). Moreover, even when found, passive genotype–environment correlation often does not explain the parenting–child outcome association in full, indicating that socialization effects are likely also present. For example, in a longitudinal genome-wide association study, the links between parenting dimensions in several domains (guided learning, reciprocity, group participation) at ages 5–12 years and children's educational attainment at 18 years was reduced when genetic influences were taken into account, indicating a passive genotype–environment correlation; nevertheless, the parenting–child outcome associations remained significant even after accounting for genetic variation, indicating a socialization effect (Wertz et al., 2020). Moreover, there was evidence for what the authors termed "genetic nurture": mothers' genetic makeup predicted their parenting (particularly cognitive stimulation, reflecting the guided learning domain), which, in turn, predicted children's subsequent educational attainment. Wertz et al. (p. 1745) concluded that "when interpreting parents' effects on children, environmentalists must consider genetic transmission, but geneticists must also consider environmental transmission."

8.3.4 Monozygotic Twin Differences Studies: Compelling Evidence for Socialization Influences

A design that is particularly effective for demonstrating socialization effects is comparing the parenting (or other socialization experiences) of identical twins and examining whether differences between the twins in these experiences contribute to differences between them in relevant child outcomes. Even when twins grow up in the same home, they do not necessarily experience the same parenting: parents and other socialization agents can treat each twin differently. Because monozygotic twins share 100 percent of their genes, associations between the twins' differential socialization experiences and differential outcomes reflect uniquely environmental effects. Using this methodology, Caspi et al. (2004) showed that the twin experiencing heightened emotional negativity and reduced warmth and acceptance from the mother showed greater antisocial behavior, both concurrently and longitudinally. This is strong evidence that parenting characterized by poorer caregiving in the reciprocity, control, and protection domains adversely impacts children by leading to antisocial behavior. Similarly, twins experiencing poorer parenting in the control and reciprocity domains than their twin siblings (less parental warmth and reasoning, greater parental hostility) have been found to have more anxiety problems (Chen et al., 2016), and twins experiencing poorer socialization in the reciprocity, protection, and group participation domains (less warm parenting and more emotionally upsetting exposure to community violence) show less adaptive social information processing, such as a greater tendency to endorse revenge goals in social situations (Sypher et al., 2019).

8.3.5 Children's Genes Moderate the Effects of Socialization

Another important form of genetic influence on socialization involves "genotype-environment interactions" (Avinun & Knafo-Noam, 2015). Such interactions reflect the fact that children's genes can modulate the manner and extent to which environmental factors, such as parenting, influence their development. In other words, the effects of parenting (or other socialization experiences) on the child depend, at least in part, on the child's genes.

One form of such interaction, "differential susceptibility" (Belsky et al., 2007), involves the idea that some children, due to their genetic makeup, are relatively unaffected by certain environmental inputs, such that variations in the quality of caregiving they experience do not particularly affect their development. In contrast, other children are highly susceptible, for better and for worse. For these children, a negative environmental input leads to a very poor outcome, but a supportive/enriching environment leads to an exceedingly positive outcome. In keeping with this model, a meta-analysis (Bakermans-Kranenburg & van Ijzendoorn, 2011) showed that, compared to children with more efficient dopamine-related genes, children with less efficient dopamine-related genes have worse outcomes (e.g., behavior problems, less prosociality) if they experience poorer parenting in the protection domain (e.g., insensitive parenting), but better outcomes than their dopamine-efficient counterparts (e.g., fewer problems, greater prosociality) if they receive nurturing caregiving.

8.3.6 Parents' Genes Influence the Effects of Children on Their Parenting

Genotype–environment interactions also affect parents. In this case, the "environment" being considered for the parent is the child's behavior or characteristics, with the parents' genes moderating how they respond to this environment – that is, the nature of their parenting behavior in response to the child. For example, Avinun and Knafo-Noam (2017) showed that children's prosocial behavior tended to increase fathers' warmth (relevant to the reciprocity domain), but only when fathers carried the Met allele of the BDNF gene. For fathers who carried only the Val allele, child prosociality and paternal warmth were unrelated. Moreover, such effects can be moderated by other variables, including parent gender (Avinun and Knafo-Noam did not find a similar effect for mothers), and even by cultural factors. For example, Avinun et al. (2018) found that Israeli fathers' behavior in the control domain, and, specifically, their tendency to respond to their children's aggression with more corporal punishment, depended on fathers' genes and religiosity. Only religious fathers who carried the Met allele of the BDNF gene showed this positive link between child aggression and corporal punishment, whereas secular fathers did not, regardless of their genes. The authors suggested that the stronger norm against the use of corporal punishment in secular, compared to religious, society suppressed secular fathers' tendency to react in this manner to their child's aggression, even when they possessed a genetic risk to do so (the Met allele).

8.3.7 Epigenetic Influences

Epigenetics is the term used to describe processes controlling the expression of genes in the DNA, but that do not change the DNA itself (Lester et al., 2016; Mileva-Seitz et al., 2016). The existence of these processes shows how genetic and environmental effects are particularly intertwined. Processes of activation and deactivation of genes occur as a result of environmental conditions that include such events as nutritional deficiencies, stress, and abuse, as well as other variations in parenting. Moreover, epigenetic changes, and their effects on gene expression, can be transmitted to the next generation. Epigenetic processes, therefore, can account for the ways in which parenting and other socialization experiences influence gene expression and thereby brain activity in children and even in grandchildren, which is then manifested in children's and grandchildren's behavior and adjustment. For example, Parade et al. (2016) found that the link between children's prior adverse life experiences pertaining to the protection, reciprocity, and control domains (e.g., maltreatment, stress) and internalizing behavior problems was partially mediated by methylation (an epigenetic effect) of relevant sites of the Glucocorticoid Receptor Gene, which is implicated in the regulation of the HPA axis. In other words, adverse socialization experiences were associated with increased methylation of parts of this gene, which in turn predicted greater internalizing problems. Beach et al. (2015) found that more supportive parenting in the protection, reciprocity, and control domains during adolescence was associated with better physical health in young adulthood, with this effect partially mediated by level of methylation in gene sites relevant to the immune system. The study of epigenetic processes in human behavior is still at an early stage; future work will shed additional light regarding the involvement of epigenetic processes in the different domains of socialization.

9 Some Final Thoughts

In this Element we have surveyed a large research literature dating back almost a century and have attempted to show how current views of socialization have emerged from that beginning. Although there are frequent complaints from those who are interested in children's socialization that the data are confusing and the recommendations for successful socialization contradictory, we have argued that thinking of socialization in terms of domains brings order to the field. Features of these domains, we suggest, also appear in the cultural and biological underpinnings of the socialization process. Children are in different states at a given time and the current state determines what is an appropriate response for the agent of socialization to make. Crying children should be picked up and comforted when they are in the protection domain but not when they are in the control domain. Complying with children's reasonable requests is important because it makes children more likely to comply willingly with parents' reasonable requests; that does not mean that parental compliance is necessary in all situations. Praise should be used sparingly, either as a support in the guided learning domain or as a way of building children's positive perceptions of themselves. Using it as a reward to increase the probability of a particular behavior occurring in the future may be counterproductive. Real-life situations are of course complex and may at times involve more than one domain or an interplay between domains (see Grusec & Davidov, 2010). Thus, domains can be thought of as elements that may appear in different constellations. Nevertheless, whether there is one or more than one domain operative, understanding the characteristics of each domain can help make sense of caregiving situations and lead to more effective responding.

Most socialization research has focused on modifying behavior that either runs counter to the values and attitudes socialization agents hope to instill (the control domain), or that arises when children are distressed and need to be soothed or to be taught to self-soothe (the protection domain). The focus on these two domains is at least in part because antisocial behaviors demand immediate attention – as, indeed, does a child's distress and upset. Other approaches to socialization, we would suggest, deserve more research attention, including accommodation of a child's reasonable requests (reciprocity), the use of teaching moments (guided learning), and encouragement of the human desire to be like other members of the social group (group participation). These occasions are less demanding of an immediate response but may, in fact, be more fruitful in their long-term effects because they do not occur in what is often a highly emotionally charged context. This hypothesis remains to be tested.

There are, of course, features of socialization that may cut across all, or nearly all, domains. These include perspective-taking, autonomy support, acceptance, and consistency. Being able to take a child's perspective helps in identifying the domain or domains at play so that appropriate action can be taken. Autonomy support reduces resistance and facilitates the child's openness to be influenced by the socialization agent. Parental acceptance provides a context in which children see socialization interventions as being in their best interest. Consistency is necessary so that messages are heard correctly. All of these are central as agents of socialization undertake the most important job there is – assisting children in being able to function successfully and productively in the social world. Indeed, investing in the next generation and the passing on of experience is what gives meaning to existence.

References

Abramovitch, R., Corter, C., Pepler, D. J., & Stanhope, L. (1986). Sibling and peer interaction: A final follow-up and a comparison. *Child Development, 57* (1), 217–229. https://doi.org/10.2307/1130653

Ainsworth, M. D. S., & Bell, S. M. (1970). Attachment, exploration, and separation: Illustrated by the behavior of one-year-olds in a Strange Situation. *Child Development, 41*(1), 49. https://doi.org/10.2307/1127388

Ainsworth, M. D. S., Blehar, M. C., Waters, E., & Wall, S. (1978). *Patterns of attachment: A psychological study of the strange situation.* Lawrence Erlbaum.

Aksan, N., Kochanska, G., & Ortmann, M. R. (2006). Mutually responsive orientation between parents and their young children: Toward methodological advances in the science of relationships. *Developmental Psychology, 42*(5), 833–848. https://doi.org/10.1037/0012-1649.42.5.833

Avinun, R., Davidov, M., Mankuta, D., & Knafo-Noam, A. (2018). Predicting the use of corporal punishment: Child aggression, parent religiosity, and the BDNF gene. *Aggressive Behavior, 44*(2), 165–175. https://doi.org/10.1002/ab.21740

Avinun, R., & Knafo-Noam, A. (2015). Socialization, genetics and their interplay in development. In J. E. Grusec & P. D. Hastings (Eds.), *Handbook of socialization: Theory and research* (2nd ed., pp. 347–371). Guilford Press.

Avinun, R., & Knafo-Noam, A. (2017). Parental brain-derived neurotrophic factor genotype, child prosociality, and their interaction as predictors of parents' warmth. *Brain and Behavior, 7*(5), 1–11. https://doi.org/10.1002/brb3.685

Ayllon, T., & Michael, J. (1959). The psychiatric nurse as a behavioral engineer. *Journal of the Experimental Analysis of Behavior, 2*(4), 323–334. https://doi.org/10.1901/jeab.1959.2-323

Ayoub, M., Briley, D. A., Grotzinger, A., et al. (2019). Genetic and environmental associations between child personality and parenting. *Social Psychological and Personality Science, 10*(6), 711–721. https://doi.org/10.1177/1948550618784890

Azmitia, M., & Hesser, J. (1993). Why siblings are important agents of cognitive development: A comparison of siblings and peers. *Child Development, 64*(2), 430–444. https://doi.org/10.1111/j.1467-8624.1993.tb02919.x

Bakermans-Kranenburg, M. J., & van Ijzendoorn, M. H. (2011). Differential susceptibility to rearing environment depending on dopamine-related genes:

New evidence and a meta-analysis. *Development and Psychopathology, 23* (1), 39–52. https://doi.org/10.1017/S0954579410000635

Baldwin, A. L. (1955). *Behavior and development in childhood.* Dryden Press.

Bandura, A. (1977). Self-efficacy: Toward a unifying theory of behavioral changes. *Psychological Review, 84*(2), 191–215.

Bandura, A. (1986). *Social foundations of thought and action: A social cognitive theory.* Prentice-Hall, Inc.

Bandura, A., & Walters, R. H. (1963). *Social learning and personality development.* Holt, Rinehart, & Winston.

Bank, L., Patterson, G. R., & Reid, J. B. (1996). Negative sibling interaction patterns as predictors of later adjustment problems in adolescent and young adult males. In G. H. Brody (Ed.), *Sibling relationships: Their causes and consequences* (pp. 197–229). Ablex Publishing.

Barber, B. K. (1996). Parental psychological control: Revisiting a neglected construct. *Child Development, 67*(6), 3296–3319. https://doi.org/10.1111/j .1467-8624.1996.tb01915.x

Barber, B. K., & Harmon, E. L. (2002). Violating the self: Parental psychological control of children and adolescents. In B. K. Barber (Ed.), *Intrusive parenting: How psychological control affects children and adolescents* (pp. 15–52). American Psychological Association. https://doi .org/https://doi.org/10.1037/10422-002

Barni, D., Ranieri, S., Scabini, E., & Rosnati, R. (2011). Value transmission in the family: Do adolescents accept the values their parents want to transmit? *Journal of Moral Education, 40* (1), 105–121. https://doi.org/10.1080 /03057240.2011.553797

Bartels, A., & Zeki, S. (2004). The neural correlates of maternal and romantic love. *NeuroImage, 21*(3), 1155–1166. https://doi.org/10.1016/j .neuroimage.2003.11.003

Baumrind, D. (1971). *Current patterns of parental authority. Developmental Psychology, 4*(1, Pt.2), 1–103. https://doi.org/10.1037/h0030372

Baumrind, D. (2012). Differentiating between confrontive and coercive kinds of parental power-assertive disciplinary practices. *Human Development, 55* (2), 35–51. https://doi.org/10.1159/000337962

Baumrind, D., & Thompson, R. A. (2002). The ethics of parenting. In M. H. Bornstein (Ed.), *Handbook of parenting: Practical issues in parenting* (2nd ed., pp. 3–34). Erlbaum.

Beach, S. R. H., Lei, M. K., Brody, G. H., & Dogan, M. V. (2015). Higher levels of protective parenting are associated with better young adult health: Exploration of mediation through epigenetic influences on pro-inflammatory processes. *Frontiers in Psychology*, 6(May), 1–11. https://doi.org/10.3389 /fpsyg.2015.00676

Bell, R. Q. (1968). A reinterpretation of the direction of effects in studies of socialization. *Psychological Review*, *75*(2), 81–95.

Belsky, J., Bakermans-Kranenburg, M. J., & Van Ijzendoorn, M. H. (2007). For better and for worse: Differential susceptibility to environmental influences. *Current Directions in Psychological Science*, *16*(6), 300–304. https://doi.org /10.1111/j.1467-8721.2007.00525.x

Belsky, J., & Haan, M. De. (2011). Annual research review: Parenting and children's brain development: The end of the beginning. *Journal of Child Psychology and Psychiatry*, *52*(4), 409–428. https://doi.org/10.1111/j.1469 -7610.2010.02281.x

Bijou, S. W., & Baer, D. M. (1961). *Child development: A systematic and empirical theory (Vol 1)*. Appleton-Century-Crofts. https://doi.org/10.1037 /11139-000

Boehm, C. (2000). Conflict and the evolution of social control. *Journal of Consciousness Studies*, *7*(1–2), 79–101.

Bokhorst, C. L., Sumter, S. R., & Westenberg, P. M. (2010). Social support from parents, friends, classmates, and teachers in children and adolescents aged 9 to 18 years: Who is perceived as most supportive? *Social Development*, *19* (2), 417–426. https://doi.org/10.1111/j.1467-9507.2009.00540.x

Bornstein, M. H. (2009). Toward a model of culture↔parent↔child transactions. In A. Sameroff (Ed.), *The transactional model of development: How children and contexts shape each other* (pp. 139–161). American Psychological Association. https://doi.org/10.1037/11877-008

Bornstein, M. H., Hahn, C. S., Bell, C., et al. (2006). Stability in cognition across early childhood: A developmental cascade. *Psychological Science*, *17* (2), 151–158. https://doi.org/10.1111/j.1467-9280.2006.01678.x

Bornstein, M. H., & Lansford, J. E. (2019). Culture and family functioning. In B. H. Fiese, M. Celano, K. Deater-Deckard, E. N. Jouriles, & M. A. Whisman (Eds.), *APA handbook of contemporary family psychology: Applications and broad impact of family psychology, Vol. 2* (pp. 417–436). American Psychological Association. https://doi.org/10.1037/0000100-026

Bornstein, M. H., Putnick, D. L., Rigo, P., et al. (2017). Neurobiology of culturally common maternal responses to infant cry. *Proceedings of the National Academy of Sciences of the United States of America*, *114*(45), E9465–E9473. https://doi.org/10.1073/pnas.1712022114

Bornstein, M. H., & Tamis-Lemonda, C. S. (1997). Maternal responsiveness and infant mental abilities: Specific predictive relations. *Infant Behavior and Development*, *20*(3), 283–296. https://doi.org/10.1016/S0163-6383(97)90001-1

Bowlby, J. (1958). The nature of the child's tie to his mother. *The International Journal of Psycho-Analysis, 39*(5), 350–373.

Bowlby, J. (1973). *Attachment and loss: Vol. 2. Separation: Anxiety and anger.* Basic Books.

Bowlby, J. (1982). Attachment and loss: Retrospect and prospect. In *American Journal of Orthopsychiatry* (Vol. 52, Issue 4, pp. 664–678). American Orthopsychiatric Association, Inc. https://doi.org/10.1111/j.1939-0025.1982.tb01456.x

Brewer, M. B. (1999). The psychology of prejudice: Ingroup love and outgroup hate? *Journal of Social Issues, 55*(3), 429–444. https://doi.org/10.1111/0022-4537.00126

Bronfenbrenner, U. (1977). Toward an experimental ecology of human development. *American Psychologist, 32*(7), 513–531. https://doi.org/10.1037/0003-066X.32.7.513

Brown, J. R., & Dunn, J. (1992). Talk with your mother or your sibling? Developmental changes in early family conversations about feelings. *Child Development, 63*(2), 336–349. https://doi.org/10.1111/j.1467-8624.1992.tb01631.x

Brownell, C. A., Svetlova, M., Anderson, R., Nichols, S. R., & Drummond, J. (2013). Socialization of early prosocial behavior: Parents' talk about emotions is associated with sharing and helping in toddlers. *Infancy, 18*(1), 91–119. https://doi.org/10.1111/j.1532-7078.2012.00125.x

Bryan, C. J., Master, A., & Walton, G. M. (2014). "Helping" versus "being a helper": Invoking the self to increase helping in young children. *Child Development, 85*(5), 1836–1842. https://doi.org/10.1111/cdev.12244

Bugental, D. B. (2000). Acquisition of the algorithms of social life: A domain-based approach. *Psychological Bulletin, 126*(2), 187–219. https://doi.org/10.1037/0033-2909.126.2.187

Bugental, D. B., & Corpuz, R. (2019). Parental attributions. In M. H. Bornstein (Ed.), *Handbook of parenting: Volume 3: Being and becoming a parent* (3rd ed., pp. 722–761). Routledge.

Bugental, D. B., Corpuz, R., & Beaulieu, D. A. (2015). An evolutionary approach to socialization. In J. E. Grusec & P. D. Hastings (Eds.), *Handbook of socialization: Theory and research* (2nd ed., pp. 325–346). Guilford.

Bugental, D. B., Corpuz, R., & Schwartz, A. (2012). Preventing children's aggression: Outcomes of an early intervention. *Developmental Psychology, 48*(5), 1443–1449. https://doi.org/10.1037/a0027303

Bugental, D. B., Ellerson, P. C., Lin, E. K., et al. (2002). A cognitive approach to child abuse prevention. *Journal of Family Psychology, 16*(3), 243–258. https://doi.org/10.1037/0893-3200.16.3.243

Bugental, D. B., & Goodnow, J. J. (1998). Socialization processes. In W. Damon, R. M. Lerner & N. Eisenberg (Eds.), *Handbook of child psychology: Vol. 3. Social, emotional, and personality development* (5th ed., pp. 389–462). Wiley.

Bugental, D. B., & Grusec, J. E. (2006). Socialization processes. In W. Damon, R. M. Lerner & N. Eisenberg (Eds.), *Handbook of child psychology: Vol. 3. Social, emotional, and personality development* (6th ed., pp. 366–428). Wiley.

Buss, A. R. (1975). The emerging field of the sociology of psychological knowledge. *American Psychologist, 30*(10), 988–1002. https://doi.org/10.1037/0003-066x.30.10.988

Carter, C. S. (2014). Oxytocin pathways and the evolution of human behavior. *Annual Review of Psychology, 65*, 17–39. https://doi.org/10.1146/annurev-psych-010213-115110

Caspi, A., Moffitt, T. E., Morgan, J., et al. (2004). Maternal expressed emotion predicts children's antisocial behavior problems: Using monozygotic-twin differences to identify environmental effects on behavioral development. *Developmental Psychology, 40*(2), 149–161. https://doi.org/10.1037/0012-1649.40.2.149

Cassidy, K. W., Fineberg, D. S., Brown, K., & Perkins, A. (2005). Theory of mind may be contagious, but you don't catch it from your twin. *Child Development, 76*(1), 97–106. https://doi.org/10.1111/j.1467-8624.2005.00832.x

Chao, R. K. (2001). Extending research on the consequences of parenting style for Chinese Americans and European Americans. *Child Development, 72*(6), 1832–1843. https://doi.org/10.1111/1467-8624.00381

Chaparro, M. P., & Grusec, J. E. (2016). Neuroticism moderates the relation between parenting and empathy and between empathy and prosocial behavior. *Merrill-Palmer Quarterly, 62*(2), 105–128. https://doi.org/10.13110/merrpalmquar1982.62.2.0105

Chen, J., Yu, J., & Zhang, J. (2016). Investigating unique environmental influences of parenting practices on youth anxiety: A monozygotic twin differences study. *International Journal of Behavioral Development, 40*(3), 205–212. https://doi.org/10.1177/0165025415611261

Collier, K. M., Coyne, S. M., Rasmussen, E. E., et al. (2016). Does parental mediation of media influence child outcomes? A meta-analysis on media time, aggression, substance use, and sexual behavior. *Developmental Psychology, 52*(5), 798–812. https://doi.org/10.1037/dev0000108

Coppens, A. D., Alcalá, L., Rogoff, B., & Mejía-arauz, R. (2016). Children's contributions in family Work: Two cultural paradigms. In S. Punch &

R. M. Vanderbeck (Eds.), *Families, Intergenerationality, and Peer Group Relations* (pp. 1–27). Springer. https://doi.org/10.1007/978-981-4585-92-7_11-2

Coyne, S. M., Radesky, J., Collier, K. M., et al. (2017). Parenting and digital media. *Pediatrics, 140*(Supplement 2), S112–S116. https://doi.org/10.1542/peds.2016-1758N

Criss, M. M., Shaw, D. S., & Ingoldsby, E. M. (2003). Mother–son positive synchrony in middle childhood: Relation to antisocial behavior. *Social Development, 12*(3), 379–400. https://doi.org/10.1111/1467-9507.00239

Dadds, M. R., & Tully, L. A. (2019). What is it to discipline a child: What should it be? A reanalysis of time-out from the perspective of child mental health, attachment, and trauma. *American Psychologist, 74*(7), 794–808. https://doi.org/10.1037/amp0000449

Dahl, A., Satlof-Bedrick, E. S., Hammond, S. I., et al. (2017). Explicit scaffolding increases simple helping in younger infants. *Developmental Psychology, 53*(3), 407–416. https://doi.org/10.1037/dev0000244

Davidov, M., & Atzaba-Poria, N. (2016). Maternal discipline and children's adjustment: The role of the cultural and situational context. *Social Development, 25*(1), 99–119. https://doi.org/10.1111/sode.12132

Davidov, M., Bar-Tuvia, S., Polacheck, N., & Grusec, J. E. (in press). Two forms of mother-child reciprocity and their links to children's cooperativeness. *Social Development.*

Davidov, M., & Grusec, J. E. (2006). Untangling the links of parental responsiveness to distress and warmth to child outcomes. *Child Development, 77*(1), 44–58. https://doi.org/10.1111/j.1467-8624.2006.00855.x

Davidov, M., Knafo-Noam, A., Serbin, L. A., & Moss, E. (2015). The influential child: How children affect their environment and influence their own risk and resilience. *Development and Psychopathology,* 27 (4), 947–951. https://doi.org/10.1017/S0954579415000619

Deater-Deckard, K., Bates, J. E., Dodge, K. A., & Pettit, G. S. (1996). Physical discipline among African American and European American mothers: Links to children's externalizing behaviors. *Developmental Psychology, 32*(6), 1065–1072. https://doi.org/10.1037/0012-1649.32.6.1065

Degnan, K. A., Henderson, H. A., Fox, N. A., & Rubin, K. H. (2008). Predicting social wariness in middle childhood: The moderating roles of childcare history, maternal personality and maternal behavior. *Social Development, 17*(3), 471–487. https://doi.org/10.1111/j.1467-9507.2007.00437.x

Dobewall, H., Savelieva, K., Seppälä, I., et al. (2019). Gene–environment correlations in parental emotional warmth and intolerance: Genome-wide analysis over two generations of the Young Finns Study. *Journal of Child*

Psychology and Psychiatry and Allied Disciplines, *60*(3), 277–285. https://doi.org/10.1111/jcpp.12995

Dollard, J., Miller, N. E., Doob, L. W., Mowrer, O. H., & Sears, R. R. (1939). *Frustration and aggression*. Yale University Press. https://doi.org/10.1037/10022-000

Dunn, J. (2015). Siblings. In In J. E. Grusec & P. D. Hastings (Eds.), *Handbook of socialization: Theory and research, 2nd ed.* (pp. 182–201). The Guilford Press.

Dunn, J., & Hughes, C. (2014). Family talk about moral issues: The toddler and preschool years. In C. Wainryb & H. Recchia (Eds.), *Talking about right and wrong: Parent–child conversations as contexts for moral development* (pp. 21–43). Cambridge University Press.

Dunn, J., Slomkowski, C., Beardsall, L., & Rende, R. (1994). Adjustment in middle childhood and early adolescence: Links with earlier and contemporary sibling relationships. *Journal of Child Psychology and Psychiatry*, *35*(3), 491–504. https://doi.org/10.1111/j.1469-7610.1994.tb01736.x

Durbin, D. L., Darling, N., Steinberg, L., & Brown, B. B. (1993). Parenting style and peer group membership among European-American adolescents. *Journal of Research on Adolescence*, *3*(1), 87–100. https://doi.org/10.1207/s15327795jra0301_5

Dweck, C. S. (1975). The role of expectations and attributions in the alleviation of learned helplessness. *Journal of Personality and Social Psychology*, *31*(4), 674–685. https://doi.org/10.1037/h0077149

Eisenberg, N., Fabes, R. A., Karbon, M., et al. (1996). The relations of children's dispositional prosocial behavior to emotionality, regulation, and social functioning. *Child Development*, *67*(3), 974–992. https://doi.org/10.1111/j.1467-8624.1996.tb01777.x

Eisenberg, N., Spinrad, T. L., & Knafo-Noam, A. (2015). Prosocial development. In M. E. Lamb and R. M. Lerner (Eds.), *Handbook of child psychology and developmental science: Socioemotional processes* (7th ed., vol. 3, pp. 610–656). John Wiley & Sons, Inc. https://doi.org/10.1002/9781118963418.childpsy315

Eisenberg, N., Spinrad, T. L., Taylor, Z. E., & Liew, J. (2019). Relations of inhibition and emotion-related parenting to young children's prosocial and vicariously induced distress behavior. *Child Development*, *90*(3), 846–858. https://doi.org/10.1111/cdev.12934

Eisenberg-Berg, N., & Geisheker, E. (1979). Content of preachings and power of the model/preacher: The effect on children's generosity. *Developmental Psychology*, *15*(2), 168–175. https://doi.org/10.1037/0012-1649.15.2.168

Ellis, W. E., & Zarbatany, L. (2007). Peer group status as a moderator of group influence on children's deviant, aggressive, and prosocial behavior. *Child Development, 78*(4), 1240–1254. https://doi.org/10.1111/j.1467-8624 .2007.01063.x

Ensor, R., Marks, A., Jacobs, L., & Hughes, C. (2010). Trajectories of antisocial behaviour towards siblings predict antisocial behaviour towards peers. *Journal of Child Psychology and Psychiatry, 51*(11), 1208–1216. https://doi .org/10.1111/j.1469-7610.2010.02276.x

Euser, S., Bosdriesz, J. R., Vrijhof, C. I., et al. (2020). How heritable are parental sensitivity and limit-setting? A longitudinal child-based twin study on observed parenting. *Child Development, 91*(6), 2255–2269. https://doi.org /10.1111/cdev.13365

Feldman, R. (2012). Parent-infant synchrony: A biobehavioral model of mutual influences in the formation of affiliative bonds. *Monographs of the Society for Research in Child Development, 77*(2), 42–51. https://doi.org/10.1111/j .1540-5834.2011.00660.x

Feldman, R. (2019). The social neuroendocrinology of human parenting. In M. H. Bornstein (Ed.), *Handbook of parenting. Vol. 2. Biology and ecology of parenting* (3rd ed., pp. 220–249). Routledge. https://doi.org/10.4324 /9780429401459-6

Feldman, R., & Bakermans-Kranenburg, M. J. (2017). Oxytocin: A parenting hormone. *Current Opinion in Psychology, 15*, 13–18. https://doi.org/10.1016 /j.copsyc.2017.02.011

Fernald, A., & Morikawa, H. (1993). Common themes and cultural variations in Japanese and American mothers' speech to infants. *Child Development, 64* (3), 637–656. https://doi.org/10.1111/j.1467-8624.1993.tb02933.x

Fiese, Barbara H., Tomcho, T. J., Douglas, M., et al. (2002). A review of 50 years of research on naturally occurring family routines and rituals: Cause for celebration? *Journal of Family Psychology, 16*(4), 381–390. https://doi.org /10.1037/0893-3200.16.4.381

Flinn, M. V. (2017). The human family: Evolutionary origins and adaptive significance. In M. Tibayrenc & F. J. Ayala (Eds.), *On human nature: Biology, psychology, ethics, politics, and religion* (pp. 251–262). Academic Press.

Flinn, M. V., Ward, C. V., & Noone, R. J. (2005). Hormones and the human family. In D. M. Buss (Ed.), *The handbook of evolutionary psychology* (pp. 552–580). Wiley.

Forgatch, M. S., & Gewirtz, A. H. (2017). The evolution of the Oregon model of parent management training. In J. R. Weisz & A. E. Kazdin (Eds.), *Evidence-based psychotherapies for children and adolescents* (3rd ed., pp. 85–102). Guilford Press.

Fox, N. A., & Davidson, R. J. (1987). Electroencephalogram asymmetry in response to the approach of a stranger and maternal separation in 10-month-old infants. *Developmental Psychology, 23*(2), 233–240. https://doi.org/10.1037/0012-1649.23.2.233

Frenkel, T. I., & Fox, N. A. (2015). Caregiver socialization factors influencing socioemotional development in infancy and childhood: A neuroscience perspective. In J. E. Grusec & P. D. Hastings (Eds.), *Handbook of socialization: Theory and research, 2nd ed.* (pp. 419–447). Guilford Press.

Freud, A. (1960). Discussion of Dr. John Bowlby's paper. *The Psychoanalytic Study of the Child, 15*(1), 53–62. https://doi.org/10.1080/00797308.1960.11822567

Freud, S. (1930). *Civilization and its discontents.* Hogarth Press.

Fries, A. B. W., Shirtcliff, E. A., & Pollak, S. D. (2008). Neuroendocrine dysregulation following early social deprivation in children. *Developmental Psychobiology, 50*(6), 588–599. https://doi.org/10.1002/dev.20319

Gardner, F., Ward, S., Burton, J., & Wilson, C. (2003). The role of mother-child joint play in the early development of children's conduct problems: A longitudinal observational study. *Social Development, 12*(3), 361–378. https://doi.org/10.1111/1467-9507.t01-1-00238

Gershoff, E. T., & Grogan-Kaylor, A. (2016). Spanking and child outcomes: Old controversies and new meta-analyses. *Journal of Family Psychology, 30*(4), 453–469. https://doi.org/10.1037/fam0000191

Gershoff, E. T., Grogan-Kaylor, A., Lansford, J. E., et al. (2010). Parent discipline practices in an international sample: Associations with child behaviors and moderation by perceived normativeness. *Child Development, 81*(2), 487–502. https://doi.org/10.1111/j.1467-8624.2009.01409.x

Gillies, R. M., & Ashman, A. F. (1998). Behavior and interactions of children in cooperative groups in lower and middle elementary grades. *Journal of Educational Psychology, 90*(4), 746–757.

Glatz, T., & Buchanan, C. M. (2015). Change and predictors of change in parental self-efficacy from early to middle adolescence. *Developmental Psychology, 51*(10), 1367–1379. https://doi.org/10.1037/dev0000035

Goldberg, S., Grusec, J. E., & Jenkins, J. M. (1999). Confidence in protection: Arguments for a narrow definition of attachment. *Journal of Family Psychology, 13*(4), 475–483. https://doi.org/10.1037/0893-3200.13.4.475

Goodnow, J. J. (1997). Parenting and the transmission and internalization of values: From social-cultural perspectives to within-family analyses. In J. E. Grusec & L. Kuczynski (Eds.), *Parenting and children's internalization of values: A handbook of contemporary theory.* (pp. 333–361). John Wiley & Sons Inc.

Gouveia, M. J., Carona, C., Canavarro, M. C., & Moreira, H. (2016). Self-compassion and dispositional mindfulness are associated with parenting styles and parenting stress: The mediating role of mindful parenting. *Mindfulness*, *7*(3), 700–712. https://doi.org/10.1007/s12671-016-0507-y

Grazzani, I., Ornaghi, V., Agliati, A., & Brazzelli, E. (2016). How to foster toddlers' mental-state talk, emotion understanding, and prosocial behavior: A conversation-based intervention at nursery school. *Infancy*, *21*(2), 199–227. https://doi.org/10.1111/infa.12107

Grolnick, W. S., & Pomerantz, E. M. (2009). Issues and challenges in studying parental control: Toward a new conceptualization. *Child Development Perspectives*, *3*(3), 165–170. https://doi.org/10.1111/j.1750-8606 .2009.00099.x

Grolnick, W. S., & Ryan, R. M. (1989). Parent styles associated with children's self-regulation and competence in school. *Journal of Educational Psychology*, *81*(2), 143–154. https://doi.org/10.1037/0022-0663.81.2.143

Grusec, J. E. (1992). Social learning theory and developmental psychology: The legacy of Robert Sears and Albert Bandura. *Developmental Psychology*, *28* (5), 776–786. https://doi.org/10.1037/0012-1649.28.5.776

Grusec, J. E. (2019). *Principles of effective parenting: How socialization works*. Guilford Press.

Grusec, J. E., & Davidov, M. (2010). Integrating different perspectives on socialization theory and research: A domain-specific approach. *Child Development*, *81*(3), 687–709. https://doi.org/10.1111/j.1467-8624 .2010.01426.x

Grusec, J. E., & Davidov, M. (2015). Analyzing socialization from a domain-specific perspective. In J. E. Grusec & P. D. Hastings (Eds.), *Handbook of socialization: Theory and research* (2nd ed., pp. 158–181). Guilford Press.

Grusec, J. E., & Davidov, M. (2019). Parent socialization and children's values. In M. H. Bornstein (Ed.), *Handbook of parenting: Volume 3: Being and becoming a parent* (3rd ed., pp. 762–796). Routledge.

Grusec, J. E., & Goodnow, J. J. (1994). Impact of parental discipline methods on the child's internalization of values: A reconceptualization of current points of view. *Developmental Psychology*, *30*(1), 4–19. https://doi.org/10.1037 /0012-1649.30.1.4

Grusec, J. E., Goodnow, J. J., & Cohen, L. (1996). Household work and the development of concern for others. *Developmental Psychology*, *32*(6), 999–1007. https://doi.org/10.1037/0012-1649.32.6.999

Grusec, J. E., & Redler, E. (1980). Attribution, reinforcement, and altruism: A developmental analysis. *Developmental Psychology*, *16*(5), 525–534. https://doi.org/10.1037/0012-1649.16.5.525

Grusec, J. E., Rudy, D., & Martini, T. (1997). Parenting cognitions and child outcomes: An overview and implications for children's internalization of values. In J. E. Grusec & L. Kuczynski (Eds.), *Parenting and children's internalization of values: A handbook of contemporary theory.* (pp. 259–282). John Wiley & Sons Inc.

Gunnar, M. R., & Donzella, B. (2002). Social regulation of the cortisol levels in early human development. *Psychoneuroendocrinology, 27*(1–2), 199–220.

Hamilton, W. D. (1964). Genetic evolution of social behavior. *Journal of Theoretical Biology, 7*(1), 1–52.

Hammond, S. I., & Carpendale, J. I. M. (2015). Helping children help: The relation between maternal scaffolding and children's early help. *Social Development, 24*(2), 367–383. https://doi.org/10.1111/sode.12104

Hannigan, L. J., Rijsdijk, F. V., Ganiban, J. M., et al. (2018). Shared genetic influences do not explain the association between parent–offspring relationship quality and offspring internalizing problems: Results from a Children-of-Twins study. *Psychological Medicine, 48*(4), 592–603. https://doi.org/10.1017/S0033291717001908

Harkness, S., & Super, C. M. (2002). Culture and parenting. In M. H. Bornstein (Ed.), *Handbook of parenting: Vol. 2.Biology and ecology of parenting* (2nd ed., pp. 253–280). Lawrence Erlbaum.

Harlow, H. F. (1958). The nature of love. *American Psychologist, 13*(12), 673–685. https://doi.org/10.1037/h0047884

Harris, J. R. (1995). Where is the child's environment? A group socialization theory of development. *Psychological Review, 102*(3), 458–489. https://doi.org/10.1037/0033-295X.102.3.458

Harter, S. (2006). The development of self-esteem. In M. H. Kernis (Ed.), *Self-esteem issues and answers: A sourcebook of current perspectives.* (pp. 144–150). Psychology Press.

Hartup, W. W., & Abecassis, M. (2002). Friends and enemies. In P. K. Smith & C. H. Hart (Eds.), *Blackwell handbook of childhood social development* (pp. 285–306). Blackwell.

Hastings, P. D., & Grusec, J. E. (1998). Parenting goals as organizers of responses to parent–child disagreement. *Developmental Psychology, 34*(3), 465–479. https://doi.org/10.1037/0012-1649.34.3.465

Hastings, P. D., Kahle, S., & Nuselovici, J. M. (2014). How well socially wary preschoolers fare over time depends on their parasympathetic regulation and socialization. *Child Development, 85*(4), 1586–1600. https://doi.org/10.1111/cdev.12228

Hodges, E. V. E., Boivin, M., Vitaro, F., & Bukowski, W. M. (1999). The power of friendship: Protection against an escalating cycle of peer victimization.

Developmental Psychology, 35(1), 94–101. https://doi.org/10.1037/0012-1649.35.1.94

Hoffman, M. L. (1970). Moral development. In P. H. Mussen (Ed.), *Carmichael's manual of child psychology* (2nd ed., pp. 261–360). Wiley.

Hoffman, M. L. (1982). Affect and moral development. *New Directions for Child Development*, 1982(16), 83–103. https://doi.org/10.1002/cd.23219821605

Holden, G. W., & Smith, M. M. (2019). Parenting cognitions. In M. H. Bornstein (Ed.), *Handbook of Parenting Volume 3: Being and becoming a parent* (3rd ed., pp. 681–721). Routledge.

Howe, C. (1989). Friendships in very young children: Definition and functions. In B. H. Schneider, G. Attili, J. Nadel, & R. P. Weissberg (Eds.), *Social competence in developmental perspective. NATO ASI Series (Series D: Behavioural and Social Sciences), vol. 51.* Springer. https://doi.org/https://doi.org/10.1007/978-94-009-2442-0_8

Humphreys, K. L., McGoron, L., Sheridan, M. A., et al. (2015). High-quality foster care mitigates callous-unemotional traits following early deprivation in boys: A randomized controlled trial. *Journal of the American Academy of Child and Adolescent Psychiatry, 54*(12), 977–983. https://doi.org/10.1016/j.jaac.2015.09.010

Hunter, S. C., Boyle, J. M. E., & Warden, D. (2004). Help seeking amongst child and adolescent victims of peer-aggression and bullying: The influence of school-stage, gender, victimisation, appraisal, and emotion. *British Journal of Educational Psychology, 74*(3), 375–390. https://doi.org/10.1348/0007099041552378

Jambon, M., Madigan, S., Plamondon, A., Daniel, E., & Jenkins, J. M. (2019). The development of empathic concern in siblings: A reciprocal influence model. *Child Development, 90*(5), 1598–1613. https://doi.org/10.1111/cdev.13015

Jenkins, J. M. (1992). Sibling relationships in disharmonious homes: Potential difficulties and protective effects. In F. Boer & J. Dunn (Eds.), *Children's sibling relationships: Developmental and clinical issues.* (pp. 125–138). Lawrence Erlbaum Associates, Inc.

Johnson, R. T., & Johnson, D. W. (1979). Type of task and student achievement and attitudes in interpersonal cooperation, competition, and individualization. *The Journal of Social Psychology, 108*(1), 37–48. https://doi.org/10.1080/00224545.1979.9711959

Jones, T. L., & Prinz, R. J. (2005). Potential roles of parental self-efficacy in parent and child adjustment: A review. *Clinical Psychology Review, 25*(3), 341–363. https://doi.org/https://doi.org/10.1016/j.cpr.2004.12.004

Kärnä, A., Voeten, M., Poskiparta, E., & Salmivalli, C. (2010). Vulnerable children in varying classroom contexts: Bystanders' behaviors moderate the effects of risk factors on victimization. *Merrill-Palmer Quarterly, 56* (3), 261–282.

Karos, L. K., Howe, N., & Aquan-Assee, J. (2007). Reciprocal and complementary sibling interactions, relationship quality and socio-emotional problem solving. *Infant and Child Development, 16*(6), 577–596. https://doi.org /10.1002/icd.492

Kil, H., & Grusec, J. E. (2020). Links among mothers' dispositional mindfulness, stress, perspective-taking, and mother-child interactions. *Mindfulness, 11*, 1710–1722. https://doi.org/10.1007/s12671-020-01387-6

Killen, M. (1991). Social and moral development in early childhood. In W. M. Kurtines & J. L. Gewirtz (Eds.), *Handbook of moral behavior and development, Vol. 1: Theory; Vol. 2: Research; Vol. 3: Application.* (pp. 115–138). Lawrence Erlbaum Associates, Inc.

Kitzmann, K. M., Cohen, R., & Lockwood, R. L. (2002). Are only children missing out? Comparison of the peer-related social competence of only children and siblings. *Journal of Social and Personal Relationships, 19*(3), 299–316. https://doi.org/10.1177/0265407502193001

Klahr, A. M., & Burt, S. A. (2014). Elucidating the etiology of individual differences in parenting: A meta-analysis of behavioral genetic research. *Psychological Bulletin, 140*(2), 544–586. https://doi.org/10.1037 /a0034205

Klahr, A. M., Burt, S. A., Leve, L. D., et al. (2017). Birth and adoptive parent antisocial behavior and parenting: A study of evocative gene-environment correlation. *Child Development, 88*(2), 505–513. https://doi.org/10.1111 /cdev.12619

Klein, M. (1952). The origins of transference. *International Journal of Psycho-Analysis, 33*, 433–438.

Klimes-Dougan, B., Klingbeil, D. A., & Meller, S. J. (2013). The impact of universal suicide-prevention programs on the help-seeking attitudes and behaviors of youths. *Crisis, 34*(2), 82–97. https://doi.org/10.1027/0227-5910/a000178

Knafo, A., & Schwartz, S. H. (2003). Parenting and adolescents' accuracy in perceiving parental values. *Child Development, 74*(2), 595–611. https://doi .org/10.1111/1467-8624.7402018

Kochanska, G. (1997). Mutually responsive orientation between mothers and their young children: Implications for early socialization. *Child Development, 68*(1), 94–112. https://doi.org/10.1111/j.1467-8624 .1997.tb01928.x

Kochanska, G., Aksan, N., Prisco, T. R., & Adams, E. E. (2008). Mother–child and father–child mutually responsive orientation in the first 2 years and children's outcomes at preschool age: Mechanisms of influence. *Child Development, 79* (1), 30–44. https://doi.org/10.1111/j.1467-8624.2007.01109.x

Kochanska, G., Kim, S., Boldt, L. J., & Nordling, J. K. (2013). Promoting toddlers' positive social-emotional outcomes in low-income families: A play-based experimental study. *Journal of Clinical Child and Adolescent Psychology, 42*(5), 700–712. https://doi.org/10.1080/15374416.2013.782815

Kramer, L., & Hamilton, T. N. (2019). Sibling caregiving. In M. H. Bornstein (Ed.), *Handbook of parenting, volume 3: Being and becoming a parent* (3rd ed., pp. 372–408). Routledge.

Kringelbach, M. L., Stark, E. A., Alexander, C., Bornstein, M. H., & Stein, A. (2016). On cuteness : Unlocking the parental brain and beyond. *Trends in Cognitive Sciences, 20*(7), 545–558. https://doi.org/10.1016/j .tics.2016.05.003

Kuczynski, L. (1983). Reasoning, prohibitions, and motivations for compliance. *Developmental Psychology, 19*(1), 126–134. https://doi.org/10 .1037/0012-1649.19.1.126

Kuczynski, L., & Mol, J. D. (2015). Dialectical models of socialization. *Handbook of Child Psychology and Developmental Science, 1*, 1–46. https://doi.org/10.1002/9781118963418.childpsy109

Kuppens, S., Laurent, L., Heyvaert, M., & Onghena, P. (2013). Associations between parental psychological control and relational aggression in children and adolescents: A multilevel and sequential meta-analysis. *Developmental Psychology, 49*(9), 1697–1712. https://doi.org/10.1037/a0030740

Laible, D. (2011). Does it matter if preschool children and mothers discuss positive vs. negative events during reminiscing? Links with mother-reported attachment, family emotional climate, and socioemotional development. *Social Development, 20*(2), 394–411. https://doi.org/10.1111/j.1467-9507 .2010.00584.x

Laible, D., & Panfile, T. M. (2014). Constructing moral, emotional, and relational understandings in the context of mother-child reminiscing. In C. Wainryb & H. Recchia (Eds.), *Talking about right and wrong: Parent–child conversations as contexts for moral development* (pp. 98–121). Cambridge University Press.

Lansford, J. E., Deater-Deckard, K., Dodge, K. A., Bates, J. E., & Pettit, G. S. (2004). Ethnic differences in the link between physical discipline and later adolescent externalizing behaviors. *Journal of Child Psychology and Psychiatry and Allied Disciplines, 45*(4), 801–812. https://doi.org/10.1111/j .1469-7610.2004.00273.x

Lansford, J. E., Dodge, K. A., Malone, P. S., et al. (2005). Physical discipline and children's adjustment: Cultural normativeness as a moderator. *Child Development*, *76*(6), 1234–1246. https://doi.org/10.1111/j.1467-8624 .2005.00847.x

Lansford, J. E., Godwin, J., Al-Hassan, S. M., et al. (2018). Longitudinal associations between parenting and youth adjustment in twelve cultural groups: Cultural normativeness of parenting as a moderator. *Developmental Psychology*, *54*(2), 362–377. https://doi.org/10.1037/dev0000416

Lay, K., Waters, E., & Park, K. A. (1989). Maternal responsiveness and child compliance: The role of mood as a mediator. *Child Development*, *60*(6), 1405–1411.

Leerkes, E. M., Weaver, J. M., & O'Brien, M. (2012). Differentiating maternal sensitivity to infant distress and non-distress. *Parenting*, *12*(2–3), 175–184. https://doi.org/10.1080/15295192.2012.683353

Lepper, M. R. (1983). Social control processes and the internalization of social values: An attributional perspective. In E. T. Higgins, D. N. Ruble, & W. W. Hartup (Eds.), *Social cognition and social development* (pp. 294–330). Cambridge University Press.

Lepper, M. R., Greene, D., & Nisbett, R. E. (1973). Undermining children's intrinsic interest with extrinsic reward: A test of the "overjustification" hypothesis. *Journal of Personality and Social Psychology*, *28*(1), 129–137. https://doi.org/10.1037/h0035519

Lester, B. M., Conradt, E., & Marsit, C. (2016). Introduction to the special section on epigenetics. *Child Development*, *87*(1), 29–37. https://doi.org/10 .1111/cdev.12489

Leve, L. D., Griffin, A. M., Natsuaki, M. N., et al. (2019). Longitudinal examination of pathways to peer problems in middle childhood: A siblings-reared-apart design. *Development and Psychopathology*, *31*(5), 1633–1647. https://doi.org/10.1017/S0954579419000890

Lewin, K., Lippitt, R., & White, R. K. (1939). Patterns of aggressive behavior in experimentally created "social climates." *The Journal of Social Psychology*, *10*(2), 269–299. https://doi.org/10.1080/00224545.1939.9713366

Lindsey, E. W., Cremeens, P. R., & Caldera, Y. M. (2010). Mother–child and father–child mutuality in two contexts: Consequences for young children's peer relationships. *Infant and Child Development*, *19*(2), 142–160. https://doi .org/10.1002/icd.645

Lindsey, E. W., Cremeens, P. R., Colwell, M. J., & Caldera, Y. M. (2009). The structure of parent–child dyadic synchrony in toddlerhood and children's communication competence and self-control. *Social Development*, *18*(2), 375–396. https://doi.org/10.1111/j.1467-9507.2008.00489.x

Lobel, A., Engels, R. C. M. E., Stone, L. L., Burk, W. J., & Granic, I. (2017). Video gaming and children's psychosocial wellbeing: A longitudinal study. *Journal of Youth and Adolescence*, *46*(4), 884–897. https://doi.org/10.1007/s10964-017-0646-z

Lorenz, K. A. (1970). Companions as factors in the bird's environment. In K. A. Lorenz (R. Martin [Trans.]), *Studies in animal and human behavior (Vol. 1)* (pp. 101–254). Harvard University Press. (Original work published 1935).

Lovaas, O. I., Koegel, R., Simmons, J. Q., & Long, J. S. (1973). Some generalization and follow-up measures on autistic children in behavior therapy. *Journal of Applied Behavior Analysis*, *6*(1), 131–165. https://doi.org/10.1901/jaba.1973.6-131

Lubbers, M. J., Kuyper, H., & van der Werf, M. P. C. (2009). Social comparison with friends versus non-friends. *European Journal of Social Psychology*, *39*(1), 52–68. https://doi.org/10.1002/ejsp.475

Maccoby, E. E. (1983). Let's not overattribute to the attribution process: Comments on social cognition and behavior. In E. T. Higgins, D. N. Ruble, & W. W. Hartup (Eds.), *Social cognition and social development: A sociocultural perspective* (pp. 356–370).Cambridge University Press.

Maccoby, E. E. (1984). Middle childhood in the context of the family. In W. A. Collins (Ed.), *Development during middle childhood: The years from six to twelve* (pp. 184–239). National Academy Press.

Maccoby, E. E. (2015). Historical overview of socialization research and theory. In J. E. Grusec & P. D. Hastings (Eds.), *Handbook of socialization: Theory and research* (2nd ed., pp. 3–32). Guilford Press.

Maccoby, E. E., & Martin, J. A. (1983). Socialization in the context of the family: Parent–child interaction. In P. H. Mussen & E. M. Hetherington (Eds.), *Handbook of child psychology: Vol. 4. Socialization, personality, and social development* (4th ed., pp. 1–101). Wiley.

MacDonald, K. (1992). Warmth as a developmental construct: An evolutionary analysis. *Child Development*, *63*(4), 753–773.

MacDonald, R. A. R., Miell, D., & Mitchell, L. (2002). An investigation of children's musical collaborations: The effect of friendship and age. *Psychology of Music*, *30*(2), 148–163. https://doi.org/https://doi.org/10.1177/0305735602302002

Marceau, K., Knopik, V. S., Neiderhiser, J. M., et al. (2015). Adolescent age moderates genetic and environmental influences on parent-adolescent positivity and negativity: Implications for genotype-environment correlation. *Development and Psychopathology*, *28*(1), 149–166. https://doi.org/10.1017/S0954579415000358

Masarik, A. S., & Rogers, C. R. (2019). Sibling warmth moderates the inter-generational transmission of romantic relationship hostility. *Journal of Marriage and Family, 82*(5), 1431–1443. https://doi.org/10.1111/jomf.12654

McAdams, T. A., Neiderhiser, J. M., Rijsdijk, F. V., et al. (2014). Accounting for genetic and environmental confounds in associations between parent and child characteristics: A systematic review of children-of-twins studies. *Psychological Bulletin, 140*(4), 1138–1173. https://doi.org/10.1037/a0036416

McElwain, N. L., & Booth-Laforce, C. (2006). Maternal sensitivity to infant distress and nondistress as predictors of infant-mother attachment security. *Journal of Family Psychology, 20*(2), 247–255. https://doi.org/10.1037/0893-3200.20.2.247

McHale, S. M., Bissell, J., & Kim, J.-Y. (2009). Sibling relationship, family, and genetic factors in sibling similarity in sexual risk. *Journal of Family Psychology, 23*(4), 562–572. https://doi.org/10.1037/a0014982

McHale, S. M., Updegraff, K. A., Helms-Erikson, H., & Crouter, A. C. (2001). Sibling influences on gender development in middle childhood and early adolescence: A longitudinal study. *Developmental Psychology, 37*(1), 115–125. https://doi.org/10.1037/0012-1649.37.1.115

Mendelson, M. J., & Gottlieb, L. N. (1994). Birth order and age differences in early sibling roles. *Canadian Journal of Behavioural Science/Revue Canadienne Des Sciences Du Comportement, 26*(3), 385–403. https://doi.org/10.1037/0008-400X.26.3.385

Mileva-Seitz, V. R., Bakermans-Kranenburg, M. J., & van IJzendoorn, M. H. (2016). Genetic mechanisms of parenting. *Hormones and Behavior, 77*, 211–223. https://doi.org/10.1016/j.yhbeh.2015.06.003

Miller, P. J., Fung, H., Lin, S., Chen, E. C.-H., & Boldt, B. R. (2012). How socialization happens on the ground: Narrative practices as alternate social-izing pathways in Taiwanese and European-American families. *Monographs of the Society for Research in Child Development, 77*(1), i–140. http://www.jstor.org/stable/41408750

Morelli, G. A., Rogoff, B., Oppenheim, D., & Goldsmith, D. (1992). Cultural variation in infants' sleeping arrangements: Questions of independence. *Developmental Psychology, 28*(4), 604–613.

Naylor, P. B., Petch, L., & Ali, P. A. (2011). Domestic violence: Bullying in the home. In C. P. Monks & I. Coyne (Eds.), *Bullying in different contexts.* (pp. 87–112). Cambridge University Press.

Nucci, L. P. (1984). Evaluating teachers as social agents: Students' ratings of domain appropriate and domain inappropriate teacher responses to transgres-sions. *American Educational Research Journal, 21*(2), 367–378. https://doi.org/10.3102/00028312021002367

O'Neal, E. E., & Plumert, J. M. (2014). Mother–child conversations about safety: Implications for socializing safety values in children. *Journal of Pediatric Psychology, 39*(4), 481–491. https://doi.org/10.1093/jpepsy/jsu005

Owens, J. (2004). Sleep in children: Cross-cultural perspectives. *Sleep and Biological Rhythms, 2*(3), 165–173. https://doi.org/10.1111/sbr.2004.2.issue-3

Padilla-Walker, L. M. (2007). Characteristics of mother-child interactions related to adolescents' positive values and behaviors. *Journal of Marriage and Family, 69*(3), 675–686. https://doi.org/10.1111/j.1741-3737.2007.00399.x

Parade, S. H., Ridout, K. K., Seifer, R., et al. (2016). Methylation of the glucocorticoid receptor gene promoter in preschoolers: Links with internalizing behavior problems. *Child Development, 87*(1), 86–97. https://doi.org/10.1111/cdev.12484

Parke, R. D., Roisman, G. I., & Rose, A. J. (2019). *Social development*. Wiley.

Parpal, M., & Maccoby, E. E. (1985). Maternal responsiveness and subsequent child compliance. *Child Development, 56*(5), 1326–1334. https://doi.org/10.2307/1130247

Parsons, C. E., Stark, E. A., Young, K. S., Stein, A., & Kringelbach, M. L. (2013). Understanding the human parental brain: A critical role of the orbitofrontal cortex. *Social Neuroscience, 8*(6), 525–543. https://doi.org/10.1080/17470919.2013.842610

Parsons, C. E., Young, K. S., Murray, L., Stein, A., & Kringelbach, M. L. (2010). The functional neuroanatomy of the evolving parent–infant relationship. *Progress in Neurobiology, 91*(3), 220–241. https://doi.org/10.1016/j.pneurobio.2010.03.001

Patterson, G. R. (1982). *A social learning approach: Vol. 3: Coercive family process*. Castilia Press.

Patterson, G. R. (1997). Performance models for parenting: A social interactional perspective. In J. E. Grusec & L. Kuczynski (Eds.), *Parenting and children's internalization of values: A handbook of contemporary theory* (pp. 193–226). Wiley.

Piaget, J. (1932). *The moral judgment of the child*. Routledge.

Priel, A., Djalovski, A., Zagoory-Sharon, O., & Feldman, R. (2019). Maternal depression impacts child psychopathology across the first decade of life: Oxytocin and synchrony as markers of resilience. *Journal of Child Psychology and Psychiatry, 60*(1), 30–42. https://doi.org/10.1111/jcpp.12880

Prot, S., Anderson, C. A., Gentile, D. A., et al. (2015). Media as agents of socialization. In J. E. Grusec & P. D. Hastings (Eds.), *Handbook of socialization: Theory and research, 2nd ed.* (pp. 276–300). The Guilford Press.

Puntambekar, S., & Hübscher, R. (2005). Tools for scaffolding students in a complex learning environment: What have we gained and what have we missed? *Educational Psychologist, 40*(1), 1–12. https://doi.org/https://doi.org/10.1207/s15326985ep4001_1

Recchia, H. E., & Howe, N. (2009). Associations between social understanding, sibling relationship quality, and siblings' conflict strategies and outcomes. *Child Development, 80*(5), 1564–1578. https://doi.org/10.1111/j.1467-8624.2009.01351.x

Rogoff, B., Paradise, R., Arauz, R. M., Correa-Chávez, M., & Angelillo, C. (2003). Firsthand learning through intent participation. *Annual Review of Psychology, 54*(1), 175–203. https://doi.org/10.1146/annurev.psych.54.101601.145118

Rose, A. J., Schwartz-Mette, R. A., Smith, R. L., et al. (2012). How girls and boys expect disclosure about problems will make them feel: Implications for friendships. *Child Development, 83*(3), 844–863. https://doi.org/10.1111/j.1467-8624.2012.01734.x

Roth, G., Assor, A., Niemiec, C. P., Ryan, R. M., & Deci, E. L. (2009). The emotional and academic consequences of parental conditional regard: Comparing conditional positive regard, conditional negative regard, and autonomy support as parenting practices. *Developmental Psychology, 45*(4), 1119–1142. https://doi.org/10.1037/a0015272

Rowe, D. C., Rodgers, J. L., & Meseck-Bushey, S. (1992). Sibling delinquency and the family environment: Shared and unshared influences. *Child Development, 63*(1), 59–67. https://doi.org/10.1111/j.1467-8624.1992.tb03595.x

Rudy, D., & Grusec, J. E. (2001). Correlates of authoritarian parenting in individualist and collectivist cultures and implications for understanding the transmission of values. *Journal of Cross-Cultural Psychology, 32*(2), 202–212. https://doi.org/10.1177/0022022101032002007

Rudy, D., & Grusec, J. E. (2006). Authoritarian parenting in individualist and collectivist groups: Associations with maternal emotion and cognition and children's self-esteem. *Journal of Family Psychology, 20*(1), 68–78. https://doi.org/10.1037/0893-3200.20.1.68

Ryan, R. M., & Deci, E. L. (2017). *Self-determination theory: Basic psychological needs in motivation, development, and wellness.* Guilford.

Scarr, S. (1992). Developmental theories for the 1990s: Development and individual differences. *Child Development, 63*(1), 1–19. https://doi.org/10.2307/1130897

Sears, R. R. (1951). A theoretical framework for personality and social behavior. *American Psychologist, 6*(9), 476–482. https://doi.org/10.1037/h0063671

Sears, R. R. (1963). Dependency motivation. M. R. Jones (Ed.), *Nebraska symposium on motivation*. (pp. 25–64). University of Nebraska Press.

Sears, R. R. (1975). Your ancients revisited: A history of child development. In E. M. Hetherington (Ed.), *Review of child development research (Vol. 5)* (pp. 1–73). University of Chicago Press.

Sears, R. R., Maccoby, E. E., & Levin, H. (1957). *Patterns of child rearing.* Row-Peterson.

Skinner, B. F. (1953). *Science and human behavior.* MacMillan.

Smith, P. K., Boulton, M. J., & Cowie, H. (1993). The impact of cooperative group work on ethnic relations in middle school. *School Psychology International, 14*(1), 21–42. https://doi.org/10.1177/0143034393141002

Smith, T. E. (1993). Growth in academic achievement and teaching younger siblings. *Social Psychology Quarterly, 56*(1), 77–85. http://www.jstor.com/stable/2786647

Snyder, J. J., & Patterson, G. R. (1995). Individual differences in social aggression: A test of a reinforcement model of socialization in the natural environment. *Behavior Therapy, 26*(2), 371–391. https://doi.org/10.1016/S0005-7894(05)80111-X

Stark, E. A., Stein, A., Young, K. S., Parsons, C. E., & Kringelbach, M. L. (2019). Neurobiology of human parenting. In M. H. Bornstein (Ed.), *Handbook of parenting Volume 2: Biology and ecology of parenting* (3rd ed., pp. 250–284). Routledge.

Stoneman, Z., Brody, G. H., & MacKinnon, C. E. (1986). Same-sex and cross-sex siblings: Activity choices, roles, behavior, and gender stereotypes. *Sex Roles, 15*(9), 495–511. https://doi.org/10.1007/BF00288227

Straus, M. A. (1996). Spanking and the making of a violent society. *Pediatrics, 98*(4), 837–842. http://pediatrics.aappublications.org/content/98/4/837.abstract

Sullivan, C. J. (2006). Early adolescent delinquency: Assessing the role of childhood problems, family environment, and peer pressure. *Youth Violence and Juvenile Justice, 4*(4), 291–313. https://doi.org/10.1177/1541204006292656

Super, C. M., & Harkness, S. (2002). Culture structures the environment for development. *Human Development, 45*(4), 270–274. https://doi.org/10.1159/000064988

Sypher, I., Hyde, L. W., Peckins, M. K., et al. (2019). Effects of parenting and community violence on aggression-related social goals: A monozygotic twin differences study. *Journal of Abnormal Child Psychology, 47*(6), 1001–1012. https://doi.org/10.1007/s10802-018-0506-7

Tan, P. Z., Oppenheimer, C. W., Ladouceur, C. D., Butterfield, R. D., & Silk, J. S. (2020). A review of associations between parental emotion socialization behaviors and the neural substrates of emotional reactivity and regulation in youth. *Developmental Psychology, 56*(3), 516–527. https://doi .org/http://dx.doi.org/10.1037/dev0000893

Thompson, R. A. (2016). Early attachment and later development: Reframing the questions. In J. Cassidy & P. R. Shaver (Eds.), *Handbook of attachment: Theory, research, and clinical applications* (3rd ed., pp. 330–348). Guilford Press.

Trickett, P. K., & Kuczynski, L. (1986). Children's misbehaviors and parental discipline strategies in abusive and nonabusive families. *Developmental Psychology, 22*(1), 115–123. http://dx.doi.org.myaccess.library.utoronto.ca /10.1037/0012-1649.22.1.115

Vinik, J., Almas, A., & Grusec, J. E. (2011). Mothers' knowledge of what distresses and what comforts their children predicts children's coping, empathy, and prosocial behavior. *Parenting, 11*(1), 56–71. https://doi.org/10 .1080/15295192.2011.539508

von Suchodoletz, A., Trommsdorff, G., & Heikamp, T. (2011). Linking maternal warmth and responsiveness to children's self-regulation. *Social Development, 20*(3), 486–503. https://doi.org/10.1111/j.1467-9507.2010.00588.x

Vygotsky, L. S. (1978). Interaction between learning and development. In M. Cole (Ed.), *Mind in society: The development of higher psychological processes* (pp. 79–92). Harvard University Press.

Walker, L. J., Hennig, K. H., & Krettenauer, T. (2000). Parent and peer contexts for children's moral reasoning development. *Child Development, 71*(4), 1033–1048. https://doi.org/10.1111/1467-8624.00207

Wang, M. T. Degol, J. L., & Amemiya, J. L. (2019). Older siblings as academic socialization agents for younger siblings: Developmental pathways across adolescence. *Journal of Youth and Adolescence, 8*, 1218–1233. https://doi .org/10.1007/s10964-019-01005-2

Warneken, F., & Tomasello, M. (2008). Extrinsic rewards undermine altruistic tendencies in 20-month-olds. *Developmental Psychology, 44*(6), 1785–1788. https://doi.org/10.1037/a0013860

Watson, J. B. (1925). Experimental studies on the growth of the emotions. *Pedagogical Seminary and Journal of Genetic Psychology, 32*(2), 328–348. https://doi.org/10.1080/08856559.1925.10534071

Wertz, J., Belsky, J., Moffitt, T. E., et al. (2019). Genetics of nurture: A test of the hypothesis that parents' genetics predict their observed caregiving. *Developmental Psychology, 55*(7), 1461–1472. https://doi.org/10.1037 /dev0000709

Wertz, J., Moffitt, T. E., Agnew-Blais, J., et al. (2020). Using DNA from mothers and children to study parental investment in children's educational

attainment. *Child Development*, *91*(5), 1745–1761. https://doi
.org/https://doi.org/10.1111/cdev.13329

Whiteman, S. D., McHale, S. M., & Crouter, A. C. (2007). Competing processes of sibling influence: Observational learning and sibling deidentification. *Social Development*, *16*(4), 642–661. https://doi.org/10.1111/j.1467-9507 .2007.00409.x

Williams, K. L., & Wahler, R. G. (2010). Are mindful parents more authoritative and less authoritarian? An analysis of clinic-referred mothers. *Journal of Child and Family Studies*, *19*(2), 230–235. https://doi.org/10.1007/s10826- 009-9309-3

Winnicott, D. W. (1953). Psychoses and child care. *Psychology and Psychotherapy: Theory, Research and Practice*, *26*, 68–74.

Wood, D., Bruner, J. S., & Ross, G. (1976). The role of tutoring in problem solving. *Journal of Child Psychology and Psychiatry*, *17*(2), 89–100. https:// doi.org/10.1111/j.1469-7610.1976.tb00381.x

Wright, N., Hill, J., Sharp, H., & Pickles, A. (2018). Maternal sensitivity to distress, attachment and the development of callous-unemotional traits in young children. *Journal of Child Psychology and Psychiatry and Allied Disciplines*, *59*(7), 790–800. https://doi.org/10.1111/jcpp.12867

Zukow-Goldring, P. (2002). Sibling caregiving. In *Handbook of parenting: Being and becoming a parent, Vol. 3, 2nd ed.* (2nd ed., pp. 253–286). Lawrence Erlbaum Associates Publishers.

Cambridge Elements ≡

Child Development

Marc H. Bornstein
National Institute of Child Health and Human Development, Bethesda
Institute for Fiscal Studies, London
UNICEF, New York City
Marc H. Bornstein is an Affiliate of the *Eunice Kennedy Shriver* National Institute of Child
Health and Human Development, an International Research Fellow at the Institute for Fiscal
Studies (London), and UNICEF Senior Advisor for Research for ECD Parenting Programmes.
Bornstein is President Emeritus of the Society for Research in Child Development,
Editor Emeritus of *Child Development*, and founding Editor of *Parenting: Science and
Practice*.

About the Series
Child development is a lively and engaging, yet serious and purposeful subject of
academic study that encompasses myriad of theories, methods, substantive areas,
and applied concerns. Cambridge Elements in Child Development proposes to address
all these key areas, with unique, comprehensive, and state-of-the-art treatments,
introducing readers to the primary currents of research and to original perspectives on,
or contributions to, principal issues and domains in the field.

Cambridge Elements $\equiv$

Child Development

Printed in the United States
by Baker & Taylor Publisher Services